The Witch's
Book of Spells

Quarto

First published in 2024 by Leaping Hare Press
an imprint of The Quarto Group.
1 Triptych Place 2nd Floor, 185 Park Street
London, United Kingdom
SE1 9SH

T (0)20 7700 6700
www.Quarto.com

ISBN 978-0-7112-8963-5
Ebook ISBN 978-0-7112-8962-8

10 9 8 7 6 5 4 3 2 1

Cover & interior illustrations by Viki Lester
of Forensics & Flowers
Design: Masumi Briozzo

Printed in China

MIX
Paper | Supporting
responsible forestry
FSC® C016973

The Witch's Book of Spells

SIMPLE SPELLS FOR EVERYDAY MAGICK

Witch of the Forest
Lindsay Squire

Illustrated by Viki Lester

Leaping Hare Press

Contents

PART III:
Correspondence — 172

Introduction

Whether it's from as far back as the Witch trials of the 16th and 17th century, or from social media today, Witches and spells are synonymous. As Witches through the ages have always known, magick has the power to bring change, giving those who practice it the ability to manifest their desires and be their best selves.

The spells in this book are accessible to all levels of experience, from those at the beginning of their Witchcraft journey, to those who have been practicing for a while. Some have been specially written for this book and I am also sharing spells and rituals from my own personal grimoire. At the top of each spell, you'll find the ingredients and tools you'll need, and information about the best time to practice and to cast it.

I remember when I first began practicing Witchcraft. I found a lot of spell books used ingredients I had no way of finding or purchasing, so for this book, I wanted to include spells that didn't require a huge and expensive list of ingredients. Although there are some spells that require herbs you might not be familiar with, the vast majority of the spells in this book use a mixture of ingredients you may already have in your kitchen cupboards. If not, the herbs and spices can be easily and cheaply found online or at your local supermarket. Using dried ingredients will not make a spell less effective, and the bonus with many dried herbs is they are cheaper to purchase than fresh. Witchcraft shouldn't and need not cost a fortune to practice! The spells in this book also make use of herbs that many may consider to be "weeds," such as dandelions and nettles, which are free and will be easy to forage for.

Before you get to the spells, Chapter 1 offers an introduction to spell casting. It covers practical topics, from what spells and magick are, to who can cast spells, when they should cast them, and how long they can take to work. This chapter will also give you practical skills about pre-spell practices, such as the importance of cleansing and how to cast a circle. In this book, I encourage you to use these spells either as they stand, or to adapt them to better suit your needs—do what feels right for you and your Craft within your own practice and magick.

I hope the spells and rituals in this book help to enrich your Witchcraft practices, and help you live your best life.

Much love,
Lindsay xx

PART I

An Introduction to Spell Casting

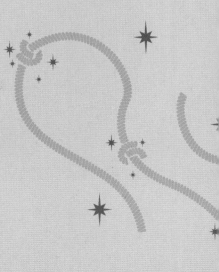

CHAPTER I

Before You Begin

Before you move on to the spells and rituals, this chapter endeavors to give you all the information and background knowledge you need to cast your own spells, as well as to answer any questions you may have about spell casting and magick.

What Are Spells & Rituals?

One of the most common characteristics of a Witch is their ability to cast spells. A spell is when we intentionally raise and direct our energy, and that of the forces of the universe, to bring about change in our life or in the world around us. You can raise this energy using the power of your will and intention, and by using ingredients such as herbs, crystals, and candles through the practice of rituals.

Spells can be complex, simple, or anything in between, and it often depends on the type of Witchcraft you practice, since this has a bearing on the kind of spell and rituals you perform within your Craft. Practitioners of ceremonial magick are known for their complex spells and rituals, though folk magick practitioners tend to cast very simple spells and rituals by comparison.

A ritual can be a religious or non-religious ceremony consisting of a sequence of different actions that are performed in a set order and in a set way. A ritual may involve words, using different ingredients such as herbs or crystals, and certain gestures, all done in a prescribed order. A spell generally consists of words that, when spoken with intention, seek to raise and direct energy to make a change to your environment. In contrast, a ritual is usually about certain actions performed in a certain way and in a particular order. Rituals tend to be more elaborate magickal workings than speaking the words of a spell, and can include calling the quarters or elements, casting a circle, and calling on spirits or deities.

WHAT IS MAGICK?

You will have noticed that in this book, I spell magick with a "k." I do this to differentiate between the magick you, I, and other Witches create from the kind of magic you see in a stage show when a magician pulls a rabbit out of a hat. Many Witches choose to use the term "magick," but it's a personal choice, so do what feels right for you.

WHO CAN CAST A SPELL?

Anyone can cast a spell or perform a ritual! You don't need to be walking a specific spiritual path or to work with any deities to cast a spell—it is all about the strength of your will and intentions. However, it's important to have the belief that your spell has the ability to bring about the change you're looking for, because nothing has a negative effect on the power of a spell more than doubt. It's also important to read about different areas of the Craft, since this will help you to become a more knowledgeable spell caster. But in practical terms, you can hone and develop your magickal skills as you practice spells themselves over time. Practice really does make perfect, since you learn from the things that went well and those that didn't.

HOW LONG DOES IT TAKE TO CAST A SPELL?

Some spells can take only a few minutes while other spells and rituals can take days, weeks, and even months to perform. The spells in this book generally take between 10–30 minutes to cast, but remember, don't rush yourself as you cast any spell or perform any ritual. A 10-minute spell can very easily turn into a 30-minute spell, and that's ok! Spell casting is a very individual practice as no two Witches are the same, so don't be afraid to take all the time you need.

WHEN CAN A SPELL BE CAST?

When it comes to casting spells, timing is key. If you align your workings with the right time of day, day of the week, or time of the year, it can help to supercharge your spell and increase its chance of success. Many Witches like to time their spell work to align with the phases of the Moon. Using the Moon in this way is a potent way to add power to your spells. Don't forget to take into account your body's own cycles and seasons and when you feel the time is right, go with your instincts and gut feelings. To help you find the right timings for your spell, see the Correspondence pages at the back of the book.

It's not a good idea to cast a spell if you're feeling unwell or when your personal energy is "off" or unbalanced. Because spell and ritual work is energy work, it can seriously affect the outcome of your spell in unknown ways if you are not feeling yourself when you cast a spell.

HOW LONG DOES IT TAKE FOR A SPELL TO WORK?

The amount of time it takes for a spell to work varies, but you're not going to see immediate visible change. A spell can work within as little as a day, while others can take weeks or even months to work, depending on the kind of spell you cast. Many Witches hold to the rule that if their spell has not begun to manifest within one lunar cycle, then it's time to check their workings for any potential issues, and even cast the spell again after they've made any changes.

The thing with spells is that you must also be willing to put in the effort with the necessary mundane actions to help manifest what you seek. You must have intention when casting a spell, but you must also do the work in your daily life to bring about the changes you want.

WORKING WITH DEITIES IN SPELLS & RITUALS

Wiccan and Pagans honor deities within their practice, but not all Witches do. It's a very personal choice, so always do what feels comfortable and right for you and your Craft. Working with deities does not guarantee spell success, nor does choosing not to work with them make you a lesser Witch. Out of the seventeen years that I've been practicing Witchcraft, it has only been in the last few years that I have felt called to work with a deity (the goddess Freyja.)

Things to Do Before You Cast a Spell

Before you perform your spell or ritual, it's important
to get into the right frame of mind as well as prepare your
tools, ingredients, and space.

GROUNDING

This is an essential skill to learn, since all magickal workings involve the movement of energy, so it's important to center yourself and ground your own personal energies before you start, as well as afterward. If you don't ground yourself properly, you can feel unbalanced within your energies, which can make you feel off-kilter. Grounding is one of the most important ways a Witch can receive energy from the earth, and to release any excess energy you may be holding onto. One way to do this before a spell is by using the following tree grounding exercise:

1. Sit somewhere quiet with your feet on the floor.
2. Breathe deeply through your nose, then out through your mouth. Make sure you are breathing deeply from your stomach, rather than from your chest.
3. Imagine you have lots of roots extending from the bottom of your feet, going deep into the earth. Visualize these roots spreading downward and outward into the soil.
4. With each exhale, visualize any unwanted energies. Move downward from your head, through your body, and out through the roots attached to your feet and into the earth. Feel any stress or tension move out of your body.
5. Keep visualizing this until you feel all the unwanted energy has been released into the earth.
6. To replenish any lost energy, visualize energies coming up from the earth, into the roots attached to your feet and into your body. Do this for as long as is needed, to replace any energy that is lost, and in order to achieve balance.

CLEANSING

Before a spell, it's important to cleanse yourself, your tools, your ingredients, and your workspace. This removes any negative or unwanted energies hanging around that may have an impact on your magickal workings. This can be done in many ways, including the following techniques:

1. Smoke cleansing: Pick and burn cleansing herbs that align with the intentions of your spell.
2. Sound cleansing: Play music or ring a bell to cleanse yourself, your tools, or your space.
3. Visualization: This is a great alternative if you don't have the ingredients needed to cleanse using other methods.
4. Crystal cleansing: Use crystals such as selenite and clear quartz to cleanse.
5. Water cleansing: Use water to cleanse water-safe tools, or yourself.
6. Moon cleansing: Place your tools in the light of the Full Moon or practice Moon bathing to cleanse yourself.

CASTING A CIRCLE

Many Witches choose to cast a circle before a spell, because it creates a protective space where negative or unwanted energies can't interfere with your workings. A circle also helps to concentrate the energy you are raising with your spell into one small space, helping to intensify its effects. Some Witches cast a circle for every spell, but there are others who tend to cast a circle only when they need extra protection, such as for banishing or binding spells.
To cast a simple circle:

1. Use salt (but not outside, since it kills plants and insects), crushed-up eggshells, candles, or protective crystals (such as black obsidian or black tourmaline) to physically mark a circle around your work space to form a protective circle. You can also visualize the circle without using any physical items.
2. Take a wand or atheme (ceremonial blade), or use your finger, to trace a clockwise circle in the air and, as you do, visualize an energetic field forming around your workspace. If it feels right, say the words, "*I cast this circle of protection around my workings and to keep out any kind of negative or unwanted energies. So mote it be.*" After you have completed your spell, to open a circle, trace the circle in a counter-clockwise direction, visualizing the energetic field you created now opening. If it feels right, say the words, "*The circle is now open but not unbroken. So mote it be.*"

Why Might a Spell Not Work?

A spell may not work for a number of reasons. Knowing about the potential pitfalls of spell casting can help you to avoid them in your own spell work. Here is a collection of the most common reasons spells don't work:

1. Your intention was not focused enough—be as specific as you can.
2. You didn't believe in your spell. You must have the belief that the spell your casting will bring about the changes you desire—doubt is an energy killer!
3. You may be expecting a spell to manifest quickly when you need to give it longer to work.
4. You have unrealistic expectations from your spell. Keep things grounded in reality.
5. You're not doing the mundane work to support your spell work. Work hard to do the practical things that will help you to achieve your magickal desires.
6. You rushed casting your spell. When performing a spell, take your time, and take care with all words and actions.
7. You cast your spell too early, without doing enough reading and research. When preparing for a spell, take time to do as much reading about it as possible so you're able to craft your spell to fit your intentions.
8. You cast a spell when you were ill or distracted. This means you're not in a good energetic place to perform a spell or ritual.

ETHICAL WITCHCRAFT

Some spells heal and others harm, but if you're looking for hexes, you won't find any in here. This book will, however provide you with spells to remove a hex or curse from yourself or someone else. This book doesn't contain spells that will affect free will either—it doesn't contain love spells that will make a specific person love you or make an ex come back. That's partly because, in my own Craft, I am not comfortable with forcing someone's free will. Instead of a spell to make someone love you, you'll find spells to attract more love into your life so that if you make a connection with someone, it will be a more sincere and natural match than one that is forced.

You must be aware of the consequences of your spell work, both good and bad. In the same way that your actions have consequences in your day-to-day life, there are consequences to your magickal actions. I personally believe that if you send ill will or negative energy into the world, it will find its way back to you eventually. So just be aware of and willing to accept the potential consequences of what you do if you choose to work with hexes, curses, or bend the will of others in your practice.

Reworking & Writing Your Own Spells

Intention is very important when writing your own spells, since you have to know clearly what you want the outcome of your spell to achieve in order to choose the right ingredients to work with.

With this in mind, in Part III of this book, you'll find a selection of Correspondence (see page 172). Spell and ritual correspondence are groupings of metaphysical and physical items that connect to specific types of magick, intentions, and magickal outcomes. They can be used to help you choose which items are aligned to the specific kind of spell you want to cast or to a ritual you want to perform. They give you the tools to be able to adapt and rework the spells in this book to suit your needs better. They contain the metaphysical properties of a range of herbs, spices, flowers, crystals, colors, as well as deities, Moon phases, and rune meanings. Knowing their properties and magickal associations means you can add or substitute ingredients to align with the intention of your spell.

If you've been practicing Witchcraft for a while, you can also use the correspondence lists in Part III to help you create your own spells from scratch, since you know what ingredients to use that align with your intention and the specific outcome you want to achieve. You can also use the correspondence in Part III to help you choose substitute ingredients if you are casting a spell from this book, but don't have all the indicated ingredients.

When writing a spell or ritual, there are several things to consider:

1. The environment you write your spells and rituals in is important. Choose a place where you're comfortable and can create the right atmosphere by burning candles, incense, or doing whatever feels right.

2. When crafting your spell or ritual, they can be as simple or as complex as you want them to be. You need to decide what form yours will take.

3. When penning your own magickal workings, you need to be very clear about your intentions and what you want to achieve. Your spell or ritual needs to be as focused as possible.

4. Think about the different outcomes of your spell if you manifest your desires. Who would it affect? What other changes could happen as a result of your spell success?

5. Consider where you are going to perform your spell or ritual. Is it a place that is symbolically linked to your magick? Will you be disturbed there?

6. Think about the tools and ingredients you'll need. Carefully select those that align with your intentions and can help you manifest your specific desires. This includes the use of sigils, runes, or any other relevant symbols.

7. Consider timing. Do you want to cast your spell at a specific time that is symbolic to your magic? Do you want to cast it on a specific day, time, or Moon phase that aligns with your intentions?

8. Think about any words you want to say or any actions you want to make. Remember, the words of a spell doesn't have to rhyme unless that's your thing!

Using Sigils in Spells & Rituals

A sigil is a magickal symbol that has been created to represent a specific intention or goal. There are many ways to create a sigil, but use the method that feels right to you. The one below is called the wheel method and is one of the easiest ways to create your own sigils, infused with your intention.

1. SET YOUR INTENTIONS

As with all sigils, it's important to be clear about your intentions before you begin. Using this method, I have found that it works better to either choose one word to represent your intentions, or a short and concise phrase just a few words long. This helps to keep the energy of your sigil focused and prevents more than one goal from being attached it. As with all spell work, keep your intentions realistic and phrase them as positively as you can. You might choose to use the present tense when phrasing your intentions, imagining you have already manifested what you want, to help attract this energy toward you. For example, "I am confident. I am protected. I have strength."

2. SIMPLIFY YOUR INTENTIONS

Once you have your chosen word or phrase, you can simplify your intentions by removing any vowels and repeated words, but this is a completely optional step. The more letters you remove, the simpler the final sigil will be.

3. CREATE YOUR SIGIL

The next step is to draw or print out a sigil wheel of your choice. Draw a dot on the first letter of the word(s) you have chosen to use and then draw a line from that dot to the next letter. Spell out the word(s), drawing a line from one letter to the next until you reach the last letter, completing your sigil.

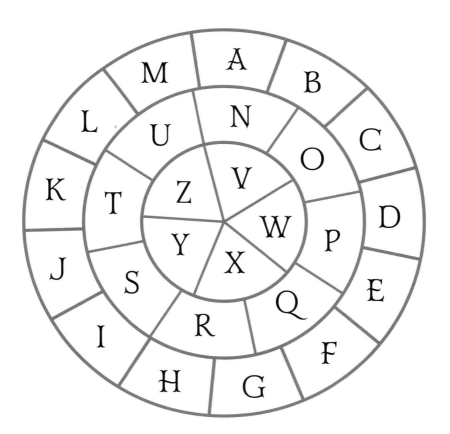

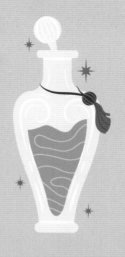

PART II

Spells & Rituals

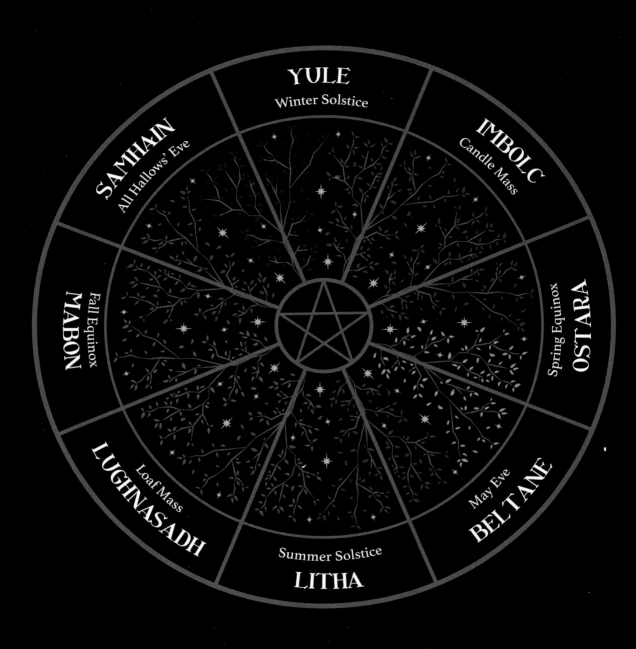

CHAPTER 2

Seasons & Sabbats

The four seasons and eight sabbats (Yule, Imbolc, Ostara, Beltane, Litha, Lughnasadh, Mabon, and Samhain) are central to many Witchcraft practices. They are a way to track the passing of time through the changing scenes of Mother Nature. In this chapter, you'll find a spell, ritual, or recipe for each Sabbat and season to help you connect to the powerful energies of what is going on in the natural world around you.

Samhain Silent Supper Ritual

Best time to practice: Samhain night

Samhain is the final harvest of the year and a time where the veil between the living and the dead is at its thinnest. It's a time to honor our ancestors and those who have gone before us. This ritual is a very traditional Pagan practice and is performed on Samhain night to honor our ancestors. It's also known as a dumb supper and is a solemn occasion where the guests do not speak throughout the meal.

INGREDIENTS
Food of your choice

TOOLS
1 white candle (to represent your ancestors)
Lighter or matches

METHOD

1. Decide what meal you will be preparing for your silent supper and gather your ingredients.
2. It is traditional for guests to bring a note to a silent supper containing the things they want to say to their loved ones, so ensure you ask them to prepare these in advance.
3. On the night of your silent supper, set a table for as many guests as will be attending, plus one extra (usually at the head of the table). This extra place is set but left vacant to represent your ancestors.
4. Prepare your meal of choice for when your guests arrive. Light the candle.
5. Once your guests have arrived and are seated at the table, hold hands for a moment to silently bless the meal.
6. Serve the meal to your guests, including the place set for your ancestors. Eat it in silence as a sign of respect.
7. When everyone has finished eating, burn the notes each guest has brought, one at a time, in the candle flame, focusing on the message each one has for their loved ones before returning to their seat.
8. To finish the meal, join hands again with everyone at the table and offer a silent prayer to the dead.

Soul Cakes Recipe

Best time to practice: Samhain night

Originating in medieval Great Britain and Ireland, soul cakes were traditionally given to children and the poor by the wealthy at Samhain in exchange for prayers for their soul, and to keep malevolent spirits away. The Christian church adopted soul cakes and they were given by churches and monasteries to the poor on All Souls Day (November 2) to honor the dead. Soul cakes are a traditional food to enjoy at this time of year.

Serves 8–10 people

INGREDIENTS

8 oz (225 g) of brown sugar
6 oz (170 g) unsalted butter
2 oz (55 g) plain Greek yogurt
1 tsp vanilla extract
4 oz (115 g) whole milk or
milk substitute
1 tsp baking powder
2 tsp pumpkin spice mix
28 oz (790 g) of strong plain flour
1 diced apple
4 oz (115 g) dried cranberries

TOOLS

Bowl
Cookie cutter
Rolling pin
Baking tray

METHOD

1. Preheat the oven to 430°F (220°C).
2. In a bowl, cream the sugar and butter together.
3. Next, add the yogurt, vanilla extract, milk, baking powder, and pumpkin spice mix to the bowl and mix the ingredients together thoroughly.
4. Add the flour a bit at a time and mix in to make a dough.
5. Fold the apple and dried cranberries into the dough.
6. Chill for 10-15 minutes in the refrigerator.
7. Roll the dough out until it's about half an inch (1 cm) thick.
8. Use a cookie or biscuit cutter to cut out the soul cakes and place them on a baking tray.
9. Make an X on the top of the cakes and brush with milk to help them turn golden brown.
10. Bake for 12 minutes.
11. Remove the soul cakes and sprinkle the tops with sugar, putting them back into the oven for a further 12-14 minutes until brown.
12. Take them out of the oven and let them cool completely before serving.

Yule Log Ritual

Best time to practice: On the eve of the Winter Solstice

Yule (or the Winter Solstice) marks the shortest day and longest night of the year. From here we move into the light half of the year, which is why this Sabbat is celebrated with lots of candles to symbolize the coming of the lighter, longer days. An ancient folk tradition at this time of year is to make a Yule log to bring into your home, which is then ritualistically burned to give warmth and to welcome the Sun's return.

INGREDIENTS
A log (any size)
Winter foliage such as leaves, pine cones, holly, ivy, and mistletoe
A length of ribbon
Scissors

TOOLS
Piece of paper and a pen
Lighter or matches

METHOD

1. Go outside and find a log that appeals to you. It can be any size but keep in mind the bigger the log, the more decoration you'll need.

2. While you're outside, gather together enough winter foliage for you to decorate your Yule log.

3. Bring the log inside and arrange the winter foliage on the log as you wish.

4. Take a piece of paper and write down your hopes, dreams, and wishes for the new year.

5. Fold up the paper and place it among the winter foliage on your Yule log. It's traditional to burn your log in a fireplace if you have one, but if you don't, you can also burn it outside in something like a fire pit. Set the log on fire and, as it burns, say this blessing: *"I welcome the Sun's return, I welcome the light and warmth, the days will get longer now from henceforth. I bless this Yule log on this night and at this hour, as I call upon the ancient power. So mote it be."*

6. Let the log completely burn down to ash.

7. It's traditional to collect the ash of the log to sprinkle it around your home for protection against malevolent spirits, but this step is optional.

Yorkshire Yule Loaf Recipe

Best time to practice: Anytime, especially around Yule

I've lived in Yorkshire, England for most of my life and this traditional Yorkshire Yule loaf recipe is one my granny used to bake a lot for me and my family around this time of year.

Serves 10–12 people

INGREDIENTS

1 oz (30 g) yeast, fresh or dried
5 fl oz (150 ml) slightly warm milk
25 oz (700 g) strong plain flour
8 oz (225 g) butter
8 oz (225 g) brown sugar
1 tsp ground cinnamon
16 oz (450 g) currents or sultanas
3 eggs
3 oz (85 g) mixed, chopped peel

TOOLS

Jug
Bowl
Dish towel
Loaf tin

METHOD

1. Dissolve the yeast in the milk in a jug and stir it in well. Leave it to prove for 25–30 minutes in a warm place.

2. Sift the flour in a bowl and then rub in the butter. Once rubbed in, add the sugar, cinnamon, the currents or sultanas, and the mixed, chopped peel.

3. When the yeast is ready, beat in three eggs.

4. Cover the mixture with a damp dish towel and put it somewhere warm so the dough can rise.

5. Grease a loaf tin with a little butter and put the dough in the tin.

6. Cover the tin with the damp dish towel again and leave to rise in the tin for another 2 hours.

7. Cook the dough for an hour at 350°F (180°C).

8. Leave to cool completely before serving.

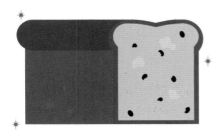

Imbolc Brigid's Cross Ritual

Brigid, also known as a Sun goddess, is honored at Imbolc, as the daylight hours get longer and we welcome back the Sun. Making her cross, also known as a Celtic Sun Wheel, is a traditional Imbolc ritual used to welcome the coming of spring. Although a Brigid's Cross is usually made from grain stalks and straw, it can also be made from paper or card.

INGREDIENTS
9 grain stalks (or thin strips of paper) about 10 (25 cm) inches long
4 pieces of string about 6 inches (15 cm) long

TOOLS
Piece of paper and a pen
Lighter or matches

METHOD

1. If you choose to use grain stalks, soak them in warm water for a few hours beforehand to soften them. Once soft enough to weave with, take them out and lay them down on a cloth to dry.
2. Before you begin, choose your intention for your cross, whether that be protection, for blessing your home, for keeping your loved ones safe, or just to honor the return of the lighter days.
3. If you are using paper to make your cross, write the intentions you have on the strips of paper. Focus these intentions as you make the cross.
4. Fold a stalk or strip of paper in half and place another stalk or strip of paper in the center of the folded stalk, holding the center between your thumb and forefinger. (Images 1, 2, and 3)
5. Turn the two stalks 90 degrees counter-clockwise so the end of the second stalk points up. (Image 4)
6. Fold a third stalk in half and put it over both parts of the second stalk. (Image 5)
7. Hold the center of the cross and turn the three stalks 90 degrees so the third stalk is pointing upward. (Image 6)
8. Fold a fourth stalk in half and place it over and between the third stalk, folded up. (Image 7)
9. Repeat the process with all 9 stalks, turning the cross around by 90 degrees for every new stalk you add until you've used them all.
10. Take the pieces of string and tie up the four ends of the cross. (Image 8)

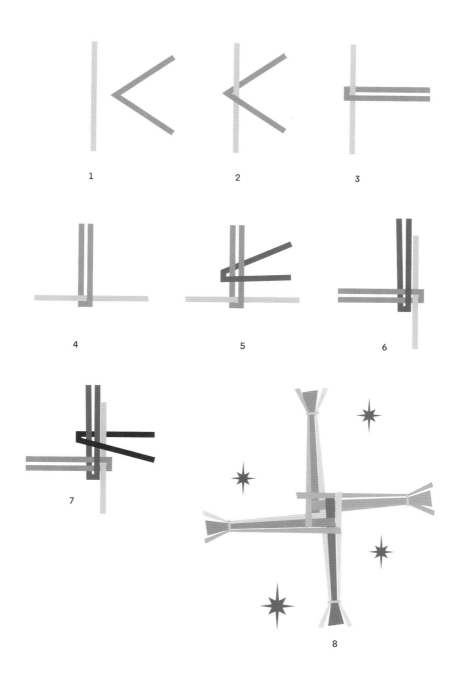

1

2

3

4

5

6

7

8

Baked Custard Recipe

The word "Imbolc" comes from the old Irish word for milk, so it's no surprise that dairy products play a big part in many Imbolc recipes. The coming of the Sun is often symbolized by the yellow yolk of the egg, meaning this baked custard is the perfect Imbolc treat.

Serves 2–3 people

INGREDIENTS
2 large eggs
16 fl oz (470 ml) milk
2 oz (55 g) sugar
Pinch of salt
Pinch of powdered or freshly grated nutmeg

TOOLS
Bowl
Whisk
4 ramekins
Large baking pan that is taller than the ramekins
Sharp knife

METHOD

1. Pre-heat the oven to 320°F (160°C).
2. In a bowl, whisk together the eggs, milk, sugar, and salt.
3. Place 4 ramekins on a large baking pan and divide the custard mixture between the ramekins.
4. Fill the pan with hot water until it almost comes to the top of the ramekins.
5. Sprinkle some powdered or grated nutmeg on the top of the custards.
6. Bake in the oven for 40–50 minutes until the custard is set. To test, place a sharp knife in the middle of one of the custards—if it comes out clean, it should be ready.

Ostara Egg Manifestation Spell

Best time to practice: Anytime around Ostara

Ostara is a time of fertility, when the natural world comes to life and blossoms around us. This manifestation spell will help you to nurture and grow your desires. A triangle can be used—the three lines represent the physical, mental, and astral planes that can magnify your intentions.

INGREDIENTS
1 egg

TOOLS
Cleansing tools
Circle casting tools (optional)
1 yellow candle (for attraction)
Piece of paper and a pen
Lighter or matches

METHOD

1. Cleanse your tools and ingredients.
2. Ground yourself, and cast a circle, if it is part of your practice.
3. On a piece of paper, draw a triangle big enough for your egg to fit inside.
4. Place the yellow candle at the top of the triangle point.
5. Take your egg and write your name or initials, and what you want to manifest in your life, on the egg.
6. When you've finished, place your egg in the middle of the triangle and light the candle.
7. Say this incantation: "*With this egg, I manifest my desires, and with this triangle, the things I seek, I acquire. So mote it be.*"
8. Let the candle burn out. Open your circle.
9. Once you've cast the spell, keep the egg in the triangle on the paper and place it somewhere safe. Keep it there until you begin to see the spell working.
10. Once you have manifested the things in your life that you cast the spell for, return the egg to the earth by burying it. This could be in your garden or any other place.

Spinach & Ham Quiche Ostara Recipe

Best time to practice: Anytime, particularly around Ostara

At the Spring Equinox, foods such as eggs, honey, sprouted greens, and baked goods are traditionally consumed to welcome the beginning of spring, making this recipe for spinach and ham quiche perfect for Ostara. If you're a vegetarian, omit the ham, perhaps substituting it for some more greens such as peas or asparagus.

Serves 8 people

INGREDIENTS

Olive oil

2 sheets of puff pasty, thawed

3 eggs, beaten

10.5 fl oz (300 ml) milk

4 oz (115 g) finely chopped spinach, frozen or fresh

2 oz (60 g) diced cooked ham

4 oz (115 g) chopped white onion

4 oz (115 g) mature cheddar

Salt and pepper to taste

TOOLS

Quiche dish

Bowl

METHOD

1. Pre-heat your oven to 340°F (170°C).

2. Rub a quiche dish with a little olive oil to stop the pastry sticking to the bottom.

3. Lay both sheets of puff pastry in the dish, trimming off any excess pastry around the rim.

4. Add the beaten eggs to a bowl with the milk, spinach, ham, onions, half of the cheese, and salt and pepper to taste.

5. Mix the ingredients together and gently pour the liquid into the quiche dish.

6. Sprinkle the remaining cheese on top of the quiche.

7. Bake for 25 minutes or until the cheese is golden brown and bubbling.

8. Let the quiche stand for 15 minutes before serving.

Beltane Incense Blend

Best time to practice: Anytime around Beltane

Beltane falls between the Spring Equinox and Summer Solstice. It's a fire festival, celebrating the beginning of summer, making it the perfect time to create your own fiery Beltane incense blend. The herbs used in this blend align with the element of Fire, so will help to form the perfect atmosphere for your Beltane celebrations.

INGREDIENTS
1 tsp dragon's blood resin
2 tsp frankincense resin
1 tsp ground cinnamon
1 tsp dried rose petals, ground
1 tsp allspice

TOOLS
Cleansing tools
Jar with a lid or airtight container
Mortar and pestle
Charcoal disc
Lighter or matches
Cauldron or heatproof dish

METHOD

1. Cleanse all your ingredients and tools.
2. Take time to ground yourself before you begin.
3. Take a mortar and pestle and grind down the dragon's blood and frankincense to a rough powder and place this in your jar or container with the ground cinnamon.
4. Grind the rose petals and allspice with the mortar and pestle and add this to your jar, mixing all the ingredients together well.
5. Place the charcoal disc into the cauldron or heatproof dish. Light the charcoal disc until it begins to spark and leave it until it begins to turn white.
6. Burn half a teaspoon of the incense blend on a charcoal disc in a cauldron or heatproof dish. Store the remains in your jar or container.

Aphrodisiac Almond Biscotti

Best time to practice: Anytime, especially around Beltane

As Beltane is a fire festival, it is often associated with sexuality. It's traditional at this time of year to eat foods considered to be aphrodisiacs. Almonds have long been known for their ability to increase feelings of sexual desire and attraction, so this biscotti recipe is the perfect fiery treat for Beltane.

Makes 8–10 biscottis

4 oz (115 g) whole almonds
3 large eggs
18 oz (510 g) all-purpose flour
4 oz (115 g) brown sugar
1 tsp baking powder
½ tsp salt
1 ½ tsp lemon zest
½ tsp vanilla extract
1 tsp almond extract

TOOLS
Baking tray
2 bowls
Whisk
Serrated knife

METHOD

1. Preheat the oven to 320°F (160°C).
2. Place the almonds on a baking tray and toast for about 10-15 minutes.
3. Crack the eggs into a bowl and whisk together.
4. Mix the flour, brown sugar, baking powder, and salt together in a bowl then add the eggs, lemon zest, vanilla extract, and almond extract and mix together.
5. When the almonds are cool, roughly chop them and add them to the mixture, making sure they are fully folded in.
6. Separate the mixture into two even parts using an extra bowl, and form them into two loaves on a baking tray.
7. Bake in the oven for 30 minutes until the loaves are golden brown.
8. Remove them from the oven and leave them to cool for 15-20 minutes.
9. With a serrated knife, cut the loaves into slices just under an inch (2.5 cm) thick.
10. Place the slices onto a baking tray and put back into the oven to bake for another 15 minutes. Turn the slices over halfway through to crisp up evenly.
11. Remove from the oven and let them cool before serving.

Litha Vitality Pouch

Best time to practice: Anytime on the Summer Solstice

Litha is the longest day of the year. From this point in the year, the days get shorter as we move toward Yule. It's a celebration of the beginning of the summer, where the Sun reaches the very height of its power. It's a time of energy, abundance, and growing crops. This pouch reflects the energy of Litha and is used to give the creator a boost of vitality and energy.

INGREDIENTS

2 fresh bay leaves (to represent fire)
Orange peel (for vitality)
1 tsp fresh mint (for energy)
1 tsp fennel seeds (for strength)
Red agate (for power)
Citrine (for vivacity)

TOOLS

Cleansing tools
Circle casting tools (optional)
Yellow or gold fabric pouch with a tie

METHOD

1. Cleanse your tools, ingredients, and space.
2. Take time to ground yourself, and cast a circle, if it is part of your practice.
3. Take the pouch and add the herbs and crystals into it. Think about the energy and vitality they will help to bring you. Repeat a mantra such as, *"I am energetic,"* or, *"Vitality is mine,"* as you fill the pouch.
4. Tie up the pouch and say this incantation: *"On this solstice, at this hour, I call upon the Sun's fiery power. Bring me vitality, fill me with energy, and banish any remaining lethargy. So mote it be."*
5. Place your pouch in the Sun to charge for an hour or two.
6. Open your circle.
7. Once charged, place the pouch on your altar and when you need a boost of energy or vitality, carry the pouch with you.

Litha Honey Cake

Best time to practice: Anytime, especially around Litha

Honey is one of the foods most associated with the Summer Solstice. This honey cake will accompany any Litha rituals you may have planned.

Serves 6–8 people

INGREDIENTS
4 oz (115 g) butter
6 oz (170 g) brown sugar
4 eggs
2 oz (55 g) honey
2 tsp vanilla extract
24 oz (680 g) all-purpose flour
½ tsp baking powder
½ tsp salt
10 fl oz (300 ml) milk

TOOLS
2 bowls
Cake tin
Knife

METHOD

1. Pre-heat the oven to 320°F (160°C).
2. Mix the butter and sugar together in a bowl until all lumps are removed.
3. Beat the eggs slowly into the mixture, adding the honey and vanilla extract.
4. In a separate bowl, combine the flour, baking powder, and salt, then slowly add them to the first bowl bit by bit, using the milk to make it into a batter.
5. Place the cake batter into a greased cake tin and bake for 15–20 minutes or until you can push a knife into the middle of the cake and it comes out clean. Be aware that honey caramelizes faster than sugar, so keep an eye on it while it is cooking.
6. Allow to cool fully before serving.

Crusty Bread Recipe

Best time to practice: Anytime, especially near Lughnasadh

Lughnasadh celebrates the grain harvest, so it's traditional to eat food containing grain, such as bread. This is the bread recipe I have used for years since I began baking with my granny when I was a child, and I always make it for Lughnasadh.

Serves 10 people

INGREDIENTS
25 oz (710 g) all-purpose flour
2 tsp salt
½ tsp yeast
12 fl oz (355 g) lukewarm water

TOOLS
Bowl
Dish towel
Baking tray

METHOD

1. Pre-heat the oven to 450°F (230°C).
2. In a bowl, combine the flour, salt, and yeast.
3. Stir in the lukewarm water until the mixture becomes a dough. Remember not to overwork the dough, since this will push out the air you need in the bread to help make it rise. The less you work it, the softer and lighter your bread will be.
4. Cover the bowl with a dish towel and place it somewhere warm until the dough doubles in size.
5. Turn out the dough onto a well-floured surface and roll it into a ball.
6. Cover the dough again and leave to rise for around 20–30 minutes.
7. Place the dough on a well-floured baking tray and bake for 8–15 minutes until the top is golden brown.
8. Remove the bread from the oven and let it cool before serving.

Lughnasadh Gratitude Crystal Grid

Best time to practice: Around Lughnasadh, or anytime you want to express gratitude

Lughnasadh marks the beginning of the first harvest. It's a time abundance and to be grateful for the fruits of the Earth and the things we have in our lives. This crystal grid will help you to express and feel gratitude, which will help to attract more abundance into your life.

INGREDIENTS
Rose quartz (for appreciation)
Citrine (for optimism)
Green aventurine (for abundance)
Clear quartz (to put things in a positive light)

TOOLS
Cleansing tools

METHOD

1. Cleanse your crystals and space.
2. Take some time to ground yourself before you begin.
3. On a flat surface where you'll be able to leave your grid out, arrange the crystals you want to use to create the shape of a Sun, so that its rays help to radiate the gratitude you want to express and feel into your life. The crystals can go in any order and the shape of the Sun can take any form that feels right to you.
4. When you create your crystal grid, it might be helpful to say a mantra throughout, such as, "*I am grateful,*" so that you can keep your intentions focused.
5. Once you've finished creating your grid and you're happy where all the crystals are placed, say: "*May the rays of my crystal grid radiate energy to help me attract more abundance into my life. May it help me to cultivate more appreciation for all that I have and be grateful for the things and people in my life. So mote it be.*"
6. Leave your grid out over Lughnasadh or until you feel the gratitude you want to feel.

Mabon Balance Ritual

Best time to practice: Around Mabon

Mabon, also known as the Fall Equinox, marks the end of summer and is a time when Witches give thanks for the harvest and prepare for the coming of winter. It's a time when the daylight and night-time hours are equal in length. Apples feature a lot in Mabon celebrations because when an apple is cut vertically, the shape of a pentagram can be seen in the flesh. Together, the two halves represent perfect balance. This apple ritual can be used to bring more balance into your own life.

INGREDIENTS
An apple

TOOLS
Cleansing tools
Circle casting tools (optional)
Knife

METHOD

1. Cleanse your tools and ingredients.
2. Ground yourself, and cast a circle, if it is part of your practice.
3. Take a sharp knife and cut your apple in half vertically to reveal the shape of the pentagram inside.
4. Hold half of the apple in each hand and say this incantation:
"*When an apple is cut in half, a star is revealed, where it was kept, quietly concealed. A star with five points to it, Earth, Air, Fire, Water, and Spirit. May it bring balance into all areas of my world, and with it a sense of well-being is unfurled. So mote it be.*"
5. Sit and focus on the ways in which you need balance in your life.
6. Open your circle.
7. When you're ready, bury the apple halves in your garden, or somewhere special outside, as an offering to Mother Earth and to nourish your sense of balance.

Apple Cinnamon Cake Recipe

Best time to practice: Anytime, especially around Mabon

During Fall, it's traditional to eat foods that are harvested around this time of year, including squash, corn, pumpkins, and root vegetables. Apples are also a very popular fruit to eat, which is why I wanted to include this recipe for apple cake.

INGREDIENTS

1 apple, sliced in half
8 oz (225g) self-raising flour
½ tsp ground cinnamon
½ tsp mixed spice (caraway, nutmeg, ground ginger, and cloves)
1 tsp baking powder
4.5 oz (125 g) butter plus 1 oz/25g of melted butter
4.5 oz (125 g) brown sugar
10.5 oz (300 g) of apples, peeled and cored
2 tsp lemon zest
2 eggs, beaten
2 tsp demerara sugar

TOOLS

8-inch (20 cm) cake tin
Sieve
Bowl

METHOD

1. Pre-heat the oven to 350°F (180°C).
2. Grease the base of an 8-inch (20 cm) cake tin.
3. Cut one apple in half and set one half aside for later. Cut the rest of the apple half into small squares.
4. Sieve the flour, cinnamon, mixed spice, and baking powder into a bowl, to remove any small lumps.
5. Rub the butter into the dried ingredients.
6. Add the brown sugar to the bowl along with the cut-up apple and lemon zest.
7. Stir in the beaten eggs, mixing all the ingredients together well, then put the mixture into the cake tin.
8. Take the remaining apple half and cut it into 6 slices. Arrange the slices on top of the cake in your chosen pattern.
9. Sprinkle the demerara sugar over the cake to create a crunchy top.
10. Bake for 30–40 minutes, until the top is golden brown.
11. Cool before serving.

Fall Tarot Ritual

Best time to practice: Throughout fall or anytime you need balance

It's not always easy to maintain a sense of balance in today's modern world. It can also be difficult to figure out where you need to bring more balance into your life, as well as the kind of balance this needs to be. This tarot ritual will help you to identify the kind of balance you're in most need of.

TOOLS
Cleansing tools
Circle casting tools (optional)
Tarot deck

METHOD

1. Cleanse your tarot deck.
2. Ground yourself, and cast a circle, if it is part of your practice.
3. Take the deck and find the Temperance card (a symbol of balance), and lay it in front of you.
4. Next, shuffle the rest of the deck. As you do, ask the deck to show you where in life you need more balance and what form this balance should take.
5. Say this incantation three times as you shuffle the cards: "*Light and dark, up and down, energies of balance I seek you now.*"
6. When you feel ready, pull one card from the deck and place it on the left side of the Temperance card. This represents the things in life you need less of.
7. Shuffle the deck again and pull another card from the deck and place it on the right-hand side of the Temperance card. This represents the things in your life you need to cultivate more of.
8. If you need more clarification, you can pull a follow-on card for each side of the Temperance card.
9. Open your circle.

Winter Reflection Oil

Best time to practice: During winter, a Waxing Moon, or on a Full Moon

Winter is part of the dark half of the year. It is the perfect time to take a cue from the natural world and take a break to rest and turn inward. This makes winter a good opportunity to practice shadow work. Shadow work is when we work with our subconscious mind to uncover any traumas we are repressing in order to bring deep and lasting healing. This oil will help to support your shadow work (see page 119 for a shadow work ritual), helping you to go deeper within in order to confront those things that stand in the way of your healing.

INGREDIENTS

5 tbsp base oil such as grapeseed or sunflower oil
2 drops rose essential oil (for worthiness), or a pinch of dried rose petals
2 drops lavender essential oil (to increase your sense of security), or a pinch of lavender buds
1 drop frankincense essential oil (to release positive vibrations), or a pinch of resin
2 drops basil essential oil (for balance and strength), or a pinch of dried basil

TOOLS

Cleansing tools
Dropper bottle

METHOD

1. Cleanse your tools, ingredients, and space.
2. Take a few moments to ground yourself.
3. Add your base oil to your bottle.
4. Add the essential oils or herbs and resin to the base oil.
5. Put the lid on the bottle and shake to mix the oils or herbs together.
6. Before you begin your shadow work, put a few drops of the oil on your hand then rub your hands together quickly to create heat and energy.
7. As you rub your hands, say these words: "*May this oil enrich my shadow work and give me the strength to confront my shadows head on. May it help me go deeper into myself, may it show me those things I am repressing, to bring deep and lasting healing to the parts of myself I am suppressing. So mote it be.*"
8. Your oil is ready to use. Store it in a cool dark place and use within three months.

Note: Small amounts of essential oils can cause irritation to very sensitive skin, even when diluted. Always perform a patch test when using this recipe for the first time.

Spring Fertility Poppet Ritual

Best time to practice: On a New Moon or Full Moon, or during springtime or ovulation

Spring is a time of fertility, where the natural world wakes up from its winter slumbers, making it a good time for spells related to fertility and new life. This fertility poppet ritual can give some extra help to those who are actively trying to conceive a baby.

INGREDIENTS

1 tsp poppy seeds (for fertility)
1 tsp sunflower seeds (to help conception)
1 tsp whole, unshelled hazelnuts or walnuts (for virility)
Crushed-up eggshells, dried, with membranes removed
Rose quartz (for healing)
Green aventurine (to support reproductive health)

TOOLS

Cleansing tools
Circle casting tools (optional)
2 pieces of green material (to symbolize fertility), large enough for the size poppet you want to make
A pen or tailor's chalk
Scissors
Needle and thread
A piece of hair from the person (yourself or another) you are casting the spell for

METHOD

1. Cleanse your ingredients and tools.
2. Ground yourself, and cast a circle, if it is part of your practice.
3. Draw the rough outline of a person on the first piece of green material. Lay this piece on the top of the second piece of material and, following the outline you've drawn, cut out the shape of the person so both pieces of material are the same size and shape.
4. With a needle and thread, sew around the edge of the shape, leaving the top of the head of the poppet unsewn. With each stitch, visualize the family you (or the person you are making it for) want to create and the future moments to be shared together.
5. Turn the poppet inside out so that all your sewing is on the inside.
6. Fill your poppet with the herbs and eggshells and a piece of your hair (or hair from the person who the spell is for). This will bind the poppet to this person.
7. Place the crystals in the poppet, putting the aventurine in the area of the womb and the rose quartz near the heart.
8. Sew up the head of the poppet to keep all the ingredients safe inside.
9. As you sew, say this incantation: "*As I sew this poppet, may fertility be mine/theirs, with every stich help me/them conceive a child as I call upon the divine. Bring me/them health and make me/them strong, for I/they have waited for this for too long. So mote it be.*"
10. Open your circle.
11. Keep the poppet in the middle of the bed, under the mattress. Once pregnant, place the poppet under a pillow until the child is born.

Summer Pyromancy Ritual

Best time to practice: During the summer or on the Summer Solstice

Summertime is a time for celebrating and enjoying the Sun and it's energy and warmth. It's a great time to practice some pyromancy, which is the art of divination by fire.

TOOLS
Cleansing tools
Circle casting tools (optional)
1 purple candle (to help you connect to your natural psychic abilities)
Lighter or matches
Piece of paper and a pen

METHOD

1. Find somewhere where there isn't a draught.
2. Cleanse your tools and space.
3. Ground yourself, and cast a circle, if it is part of your practice.
4. Place the candle around 15 inches (40 cm) away from where you're sitting and light it.
5. Sit quietly and try and enter a state of relaxed awareness. Take your time, don't rush. Allow your eyes to focus on the flame.
6. When your mind is calm and you feel ready, ask any question you want an answer to. Focus on the flame as you do so.
7. Watch how it moves and see the shapes it makes in response.
8. When you are finished, sit and write about any messages or images you saw within the flame as you focused.
9. Blow out the candle and open your circle.

- A bright, steady, and tall flame signifies a strong energy and can be a "yes" answer to your question.
- A small, unsteady, or dim flame means the energy is weak and can be interpreted as a "no."
- A flame that dances and seems to spiral can indicate problems or upcoming complications.
- A flame that flickers up brightly can signify good luck and prosperity.

CHAPTER 3

Moon Magick

The phases of the Moon play a large part of the practice of many Witches. This chapter contains spells and rituals associated with the four main phases of the Moon so that you can harness the power of the lunar energies at different times of the month.

New Moon Tarot Ritual

Best time to practice: On a New Moon

The New Moon is a time to set intentions for the new lunar cycle. This ritual will help you set your own goals for the months ahead and work out the actions you need to take to help manifest them.

INGREDIENTS

A rosemary incense stick, cone, or bundle (for cleansing)
A tarot card that represents what you want to achieve

TOOLS

Lighter or matches
Incense holder
Cleansing tools
Circle casting tools (optional)
Piece of paper and a pen
Water in a spritz bottle

METHOD

1. Light the rosemary incense or bundle and cleanse your tools and space.
2. Place the incense in an incense holder.
3. Ground yourself, and cast a circle, if it is part of your practice.
4. Take a tarot deck and choose a card that represents your intentions. For example, The Empress card for fertility or The Hanged Man card for letting go of something.
5. On a piece of paper, write in detail about your intentions for this lunar cycle and how you plan to cultivate them. Think about exactly how you want to go about this in both magickal and mundane terms, and how the energies of the tarot card represent these goals.
6. Once you've finished, fold the paper, pass it through the smoke of the rosemary incense, and then gently spritz the paper with water to cleanse it from unwanted energies that may interfere with the manifestation of your goals.
7. Place the tarot card on your altar or somewhere you can see it. It will act as a visual representation of your goals.
8. Open your circle.
9. Keep the paper with you all month as a reminder to actively manifest your intentions.
10. When you have manifested your desires, burn the piece of paper.

Waxing Moon Spoon Ritual

Best time to practice: During a Waxing Moon

The Waxing Moon is associated with attraction magick, since it's a time when the Moon grows larger in the sky as it moves closer to being full. This simple ritual will help to attract the things you desire toward you, whether that be health, luck, abundance, or protection. This ritual brings a touch of magick to your everyday routine.

INGREDIENTS
Your favorite hot drink

TOOLS
Mug
Spoon

METHOD

1. Prepare your favorite hot drink and sit somewhere comfortable.
2. Pick up your spoon and stir your drink in a counter-clockwise direction in order to remove any unwanted or negative energies that may stand in the way of attracting the things you want.
3. As you stir, say these words: "*As I stir this drink, I remove all the unwanted energy and barriers that hinder me attracting what I desire. So mote it be.*"
4. Keep stirring for as long as you feel you need to, until all this energy is gone.
5. To fill the energetic void made by the removal of this energy, stir your drink in a clockwise direction to call in attractive energy. As you stir, think about the kind of energy you want to attract (love, money, peace) and when you're ready, say these words: "*As I stir this drink, I attract into my life the energy I seek (state your intentions here). I am a magnet to the things I desire. So mote it be.*"
6. Enjoy your drink!

Full Moon Release Ritual

The Full Moon is traditionally a time for release and letting go of the feelings, emotions, and things that no longer nourish your highest good. This ritual will help you to release those things in your life that no longer serve you.

INGREDIENTS
Selenite (to bring lunar light into your ritual)
Moonstone (to harness the power of the Full Moon)
Labradorite (for positive transformation)
Clear quartz (for healing and power)

TOOLS
Cleansing tools
Circle casting tools (optional)
Piece of paper (or a journal) and a pen

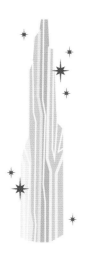

METHOD

1. Cleanse your tools, ingredients, and space.
2. Sit somewhere comfortable where you won't be disturbed.
3. Ground yourself, and cast a circle, if it is part of your practice.
4. Hold the crystals in your hands and close your eyes to help you to connect to the Moon's energy.
5. Try to allow your mind to calm down and find peace. If thoughts keep popping into your head, let them pass through—don't try and hold onto them. You could visualize putting your thoughts on a leaf and then watching it float away down a river or stream.
6. When you feel ready, lay out the crystals before you. Take your journal or piece of paper and make a list of as many affirmations as you can think of based on what you want to release at this time. Write them in the present tense, as if you have already released the things you want to let go of in order to help manifest them. These affirmations could include: "I am free from. . . . "; "I have released. . . from my life"; "I forgive myself for. . . "; "I am cleansed from. . ."; or, "I have let go of. . . ."
7. When you've finished, reflect on what you have written.
8. Open your circle.
9. Carry the crystals around with you for a full lunar cycle, to harness the power of the Full Moon and to aid the release of the things you wrote about in your affirmations.

Waning Moon Decrease Bath Ritual

Best time to practice: During a Waning Moon, or anytime you feel the need to decrease negative issues in your life

The word "waning" means to get smaller or shrink, which is what the Moon appears to do in the sky during this Moon phase. During this time, this bath soak will help you slow down, go inward, and reflect. The Epsom salts will help to cleanse you of those things you seek to decrease and release.

INGREDIENTS

Your favorite calming incense
1 cup Epsom salts
1 tsp dried lavender (for relaxation and peace)
1 tsp dried chamomile (to calm the nervous system)
1 tsp fresh rosemary (for mental clarity)

TOOLS

Cleansing tools
Lighter or matches
Incense holder
Tea-light candles
Fabric pouch made from thin material such as muslin or organza
Piece of paper and a pen

METHOD

1. Cleanse your ingredients, tools, and space.
2. Take some time to ground your energies.
3. Run a hot bath, light your incense, and place it in a holder. Place the candles around the bath or room.
4. Once the bath is full, add the Epsom salts to the water.
5. Add the herbs to a fabric pouch.
6. Copy the following runes below on a piece of paper, to spell out the word "decrease." Fold up the paper and place it in your pouch.

7. Put the pouch into your bath so the herbs can infuse the water.
8. Get into the bath and lay down for a few moments as you clear your mind and focus on your breathing. When you feel calm, think about the things in your life that you want to reduce and release.
9. When you're ready, say this incantation: *"As I reflect and go inward, I identify the things in my life that need to decrease, shrinking them down to nothing before my eyes, I have the power to release. With the power of the waning of the Moon, the inner things that affect me get smaller, and with this energetic release, I can stand taller. So mote it be."*
10. Enjoy your bath for as long as you want to.
11. Afterward, extinguish the candles and incense, if still alight.

Note: Rosemary should be avoided by people with epilepsy.

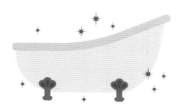

CHAPTER 4

Money, Prosperity & Abundance

Spells and rituals associated with money and prosperity are a common form of magick. Prosperity and abundance can also be associated with other forms of wealth in your life, such as peace or success. This chapter contains a range of different spells and rituals that seek to draw all kinds of wealth, abundance, and prosperity toward you.

A Seven-Day Spell to Grow Finances

This spell was adapted from Cassandra Eason's *1001 Spells*, No 63. Cast over seven days, it will help you to grow your savings and improve your financial situation.

INGREDIENTS
7 silver coins in the currency of your country
A basil plant in a pot (for wealth)

TOOLS
Cleansing tools

METHOD

1. Cleanse your ingredients and workspace.
2. Ground yourself.
3. On the first night of the spell, take one of the silver coins and bury it in the soil of the basil plant.
4. Say these words: *"I bury this coin deep in the soil so that my money will grow and prosper. So mote it be."*
5. At the same time of day for the following six days, bury one coin each day in the soil of the basil pot and repeat the words above.
6. Continue to care for the plant and, as it grows and thrives, so will your own finances.
7. When the plant grows bigger, either repot it into a bigger pot or plant it in your garden where you can keep caring for it.

Quick Money Candle Spell

This spell is to bring a quick injection of money into your life when you're looking for a short-term solution to any money issues. Remember to be realistic with the amount you have in mind, since this spell won't make you a millionaire!

TOOLS
Cleansing tools
Circle casting tools (optional)
Knife
1 green candle (to draw money)
Lighter or matches

METHOD

1. Cleanse your tools and space.
2. Take some time to ground yourself, and cast a circle, if it is part of your practice.
3. Use a knife to carve the symbol for the currency of your country and the rune Fehu (see page 184) into the candle wax.
4. Light the candle and say these words three times: *"Money flows to me without delay. It comes quickly and directly, it's coming my way. It's coming my way today. So mote it be."*
5. Let the candle burn for a few minutes, then blow it out.
6. Open your circle.
7. If the spell doesn't work within a few days, light the candle again and repeat the words. The spell can be repeated until the money you need comes your way or until the candle completely burns out.

Abundance Tea

Best time to practice: During a Waxing Moon, on a Full Moon, or anytime you want a boost of abundance in your life

Tea drinking is an easy way to bring magick into your daily life. This tea will help to draw any kind of abundance (not just money) into your life such as peace, balance, and well-being.

INGREDIENTS

1 tsp dried dandelion flowers
(for abundance and strength)
1 tsp dried calendula flowers
(for well-being)
1 tsp dried patchouli leaf
(for manifestation)
Kettle of hot water

TOOLS

Cleansing tools
A mug
Tea ball strainer

METHOD

1. Cleanse your tools, ingredients, and space.
2. Take time to ground yourself.
3. Add the herbs to your tea ball strainer and close it securely.
4. Fill your mug with hot (but not boiling) water and add your tea ball strainer.
5. Let it steep for 5 minutes and, as it steeps, think about the kind of abundance you want to welcome into your life. You could repeat a mantra such as, "*I attract abundance,*" if it feels right to do so.
6. When the tea is ready, say: "*In my life I have more than enough, as much as this overflowing cup. As the Moon waxes and wanes, abundance flows into my life again and again. So mote it be.*"
7. Take a sip and enjoy your tea.

Note: All herbal teas must be taken with caution by anyone taking prescribed medication. Check with your medical herbalist or doctor before drinking this tea, and avoid if pregnant.

Money Bowl for Financial Stability

Best time to practice: On a Full Moon or Thursday

A money bowl is a form of magick known as representational magick. This is where you add or take away different elements of the spell regularly over time to represent a flow of energy. In this case, it symbolizes a constant flow of financial good luck and stability into your life for as long as you need it.

INGREDIENTS
1 tsp dried basil (to bring wealth)
1 tsp dried thyme (for prosperity)
1 tsp ground ginger (to stop poverty)
1 tsp ground cinnamon (to draw money)
2 star anise (to bring luck)
Turquoise (to attract wealth)
Amazonite (for abundance)
Clear quartz (to amplify the energies of other crystals)
Green aventurine (to attract good fortune)

TOOLS
Cleansing tools
Bowl
Silver coins of your choice

METHOD

1. Cleanse your tools and ingredients.
2. Ground yourself.
3. Sprinkle the herbs and spices into the bottom of your bowl, then add the star anise.
4. Arrange the crystals on top of the herbs. Each time you add one, think about your intentions for each ingredient.
5. In between the crystals, place a selection of coins. It's up to you how many you include. More money doesn't necessarily help to draw a greater level of financial stability.
6. When you've finished making up your bowl, say these words: *"May this money bowl aid the flow of money into my life. So mote it be."*
7. Leave your bowl somewhere you can easily see it, as a present reminder of your intentions. Regularly add items that represent money, wealth, and financial stability to your bowl.
8. If you reach a point where you can no longer fit any more into your bowl without it overflowing, remove some of the older items to keep the energy flowing.

Chestnut Ritual for Attracting Long-term Prosperity

Best time to practice: During a Waxing Moon, or on a Full Moon

This simple folk ritual will help to draw long-term prosperity toward you. Although it doesn't require a lot of ingredients, it is traditionally a ritual for chestnut season, which is mid-September to November in the Northern Hemisphere, and mid-March to July in the Southern Hemisphere. You can also buy chestnuts in stores all year round, which will work just as well.

INGREDIENTS
A small chestnut (to attract prosperity and wealth)

TOOLS
Cleansing tools
Paper money (any amount)
A rubber band or clear adhesive tape
Your wallet

METHOD

1. Cleanse your tools, ingredients, and space.
2. Take time to ground yourself.
3. Take a small chestnut and wrap it in the paper money, securing it with a rubber band or clear adhesive tape.
4. Rub your hands together to generate energy until your hands are warm, then hold the chestnut in both hands and say this incantation three times: *"Chestnut, chestnut draw to me, bring into my life lasting, long-term prosperity. So mote it be."*
5. Place the chestnut in your wallet to continue to draw prosperity.

Abundance Spell Jar

Best time to practice: During a Waxing Moon, or on a Full Moon, or Thursday

Using a spell jar for any intention is great for longer-lasting effects, since the energies of your spell will be released over a longer period of time. This spell jar works to bring abundance into your life.

INGREDIENTS
1 tsp ground cinnamon (to draw abundance)
1 tsp allspice (for prosperity)
1 tsp poppy seeds (for plenty)
Tiger's eye (for wealth)

TOOLS
Cleansing tools
Circle casting tools (optional)
Jar with a lid
Lighter or matches
1 green candle (to draw money)

METHOD

1. Cleanse your tools, ingredients, and space.
2. Ground yourself, and cast a circle, if it is part of your practice.
3. Add the herbs and crystals to your jar and, as you do, visualize the kind of abundance you want to attract into your life. Visualize yourself already having this abundance.
4. Seal the lid on your jar and light the green candle.
5. Drip green wax around the lid of the jar to seal in your magick. As you do, say: *"In my life abundance enters, and into my life this prosperity is centered. I attract the abundance I desire, as well as the abundance I require. So mote it be."*
6. Open your circle.
7. Place the jar where you can see it regularly or in an area that is related to the abundance you wish to draw into your life.
8. To revive your spell jar at any time, give it a shake.

Wealth Oil

Best time to practice: During the Waning or Waxing Moon

This is a great all-purpose oil to use when you want to draw wealth toward you. It can be used to anoint yourself or others, to anoint candles, or can be used in any kind of money, wealth, and prosperity spells and rituals.

INGREDIENTS

2 tsp dried basil (to attract wealth)
2 tsp dried patchouli leaves (to attract money)
2 tsp ground cinnamon (for wealth and extra power)
7 fl oz (200 ml) base oil, such as grapeseed or sunflower oil

TOOLS

Cleansing tools
Dropper bottle

METHOD

1. Cleanse your tools and ingredients.
2. Take a few moments to ground your energy.
3. Fill your bottle with a teaspoon of each of the herbs and spices.
4. Next, fill your bottle to the top with your chosen base oil.
5. As you put the lid on the bottle, say these words: *"This oil draws money into my life. It attracts the wealth I seek. So mote it be."* Leave the bottle in a warm place for about a week to allow the herbs to infuse the oil.
6. After 2 weeks, drain the herbs from the oil.
7. Add another teaspoon of each of the herbs and leave in a warm place again for another 2 weeks, to allow the new herbs to make the oil more potent.
8. As you put the lid on the bottle, repeat the same words above as you did before.
9. After 2 weeks, drain the herbs again. Now your oil is ready to use. Use within 3 months.

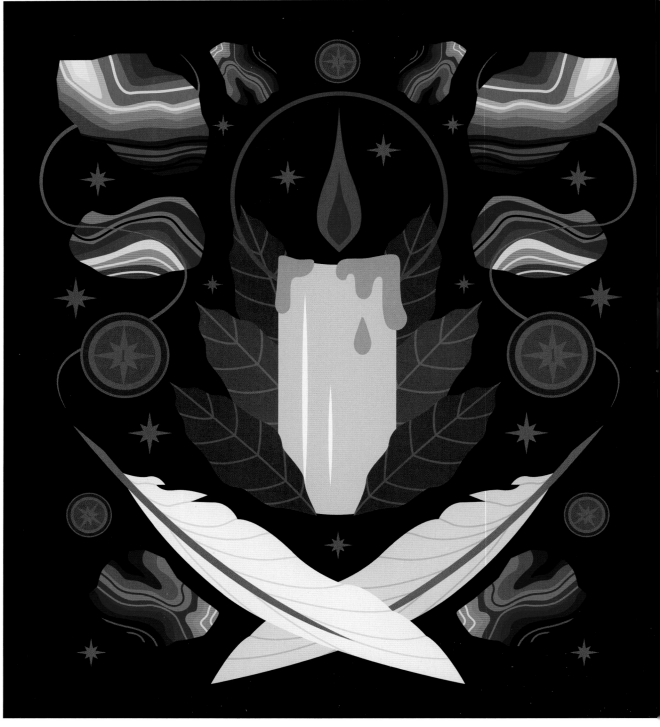

CHAPTER 5

Career, Job & Ambition

This chapter contains spells and rituals to give a magickal helping hand to all things related to your career and ambition—from landing the right job, getting a promotion or a raise, or attaining interview success, to achieving all your workplace and career goals.

Candle Spell to Find the Right Job

Best time to practice: On a New Moon, Full Moon, or a Thursday

Job hunting can be difficult, but this spell can help to bring luck and success to help you find the kind of job you're looking for.

INGREDIENTS
Carnelian (for work)
Labradorite (for ambition)
Citrine (for positivity and success)

TOOLS
Cleansing tools
Circle casting tools (optional)
1 gold candle (for success)
1 green candle (for prosperity)
1 orange candle (for good luck)
Knife

METHOD

1. Cleanse your tools, crystals, and space.
2. Ground yourself, and cast a circle, if it is part of your practice.
3. Take a knife and carve into the candles the kind of job you're looking for, being as specific as you possibly can. If there is a specific place you want to work, carve the name of the company into the wax. If you have the job title of the kind of employment you seek, carve this into the candle, too.
4. Light the candles and place the crystals around them.
5. Say this incantation: *"I look for a new job, I seek a new position, on the lookout for fresh employment, I seek this transition. As I search and look around, the right job for me shall be found. So mote it be."*
6. Let the candles burn out and open your circle.
7. Carry the crystals with you when hunting for new employment and applying for jobs.

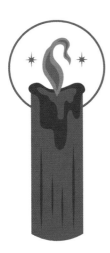

Confidence in the Workplace Charm

Best time to practice: During a Waxing Moon, or on a Full Moon, or Wednesday

The workplace can be a stressful place to be sometimes, but this spell can give you the boost of confidence you need to feel more self-assured wherever you work. This spell is great if you've just started a new job and need an injection of confidence as you get used to your new surroundings and role.

INGREDIENTS
A pinch of chamomile (to reduce stress and anxiety)
A pinch of dried thyme (for courage)
A pinch of dried jasmine (for self-esteem)

TOOLS
Cleansing tools
Your work uniform or a piece of clothing you wear to work regularly

METHOD

1. Cleanse your tools and space.
2. Ground yourself.
3. Take the item of clothing you want to charm (whether that's a uniform or your own clothes) and hold it in your hands for a moment. Visualize filling the garment with the kind of confidence you need in your place of work. You could visualize this as bright white light filling the clothes.
4. Lay the item down and sprinkle a small pinch of each of the herbs onto it. As you do, say these words: *"I attract confidence, I am self-assured, of my own abilities at work I am reassured. I know I can do what's expected of me, confidence in my work is guaranteed. So mote it be."*
5. Fold the item of clothing up and leave it to one side until you need to wear it to work.
6. When you need to wear the clothes for your job, shake off the herbs and then get dressed. As you do, say this incantation until you have put on the clothes and are ready to go to work: *"Wearing this/these (name of item), confidence will be mine in all I do at work today. So mote it be."*
7. As you wear your uniform or the piece of clothing, it will help to fill you with confidence in your abilities in your place of work.

Career Success Spell

Best time to practice: On a New Moon, Full Moon, or Sunday

This spell is to help bring a boost of success in your current job, career, or position.

INGREDIENTS
1 tsp dried basil, roughly ground (to attract job success)
1 tsp dried chamomile, roughly ground (to increase success)
1 tsp dried bay leaf, roughly ground (for good fortune)
0.2 fl oz (5 ml) base oil such as grapeseed or sunflower oil
Green aventurine (for luck in your job)
Carnelian (for renewal and creativity)
Sodalite (to boost your career)

TOOLS
Cleansing tools
Circle casting tools (optional)
1 orange candle (for careers, good fortune, and prosperity)
1 yellow candle (for success and confidence)
1 pink candle (for self-belief and self-love)
Plate
Lighter or matches
Fabric pouch with a tie

METHOD

1. Cleanse all your ingredients, tools, and space.
2. Ground yourself, and cast a circle, if it is part of your practice.
3. Use a little oil to dress your candles, rubbing them from bottom to top, in a clockwise direction to symbolize attraction.
4. Sprinkle the candles with the herb mix so they stick to the oil.
5. Stand the candles on the plate, then light the wicks. Take some time to visualize the kind of job success you want to attract, being as specific and detailed as possible.
6. When you're ready, say this incantation three times: *"Job success I seek as these words I speak, Job success will be mine and good fortune and a career boost is my design. So mote it be."*
7. Let the candle burn as you focus your attention on your situation. Picture in your head what it will be like if you already have the job success you desire. How do you feel? How will it change your life? How would things change for you in your job? Visualizing the job success as yours already is a powerful way to attract these things toward you.
8. Open your circle.
9. After the spell, place the crystals in a pouch and carry them with you at work to help you attract the success you desire.

Simmer Pot for Interview Success

Best time to practice: The night before an interview

This spell will give you a boost of confidence and self-belief so you can shine and be a big success in a job interview. It'll make sure you've got luck on your side.

INGREDIENTS
2 cinnamon sticks (for prosperity)
6 cloves (to attract abundance)
Peel of 1 orange (for success)
2 ginger roots (for good luck)
A sprig of rosemary (for inner confidence)

TOOLS
Cleansing tools
Pan

METHOD

1. Cleanse your ingredients, tools, and work space.
2. Take some time to ground yourself.
3. Place all your ingredients into the pan. Add enough water so the ingredients float.
4. Simmer on a low heat for 2 hours.
5. After this time, stand near the stove and take time to smell the aromas of the herbs and spices. Visualize the smells as a white light completely surrounding you. As you breathe this white light in, visualize yourself taking in confidence that will enable you to impress the interviewer(s). Visualize yourself getting the job and how amazing it feels, and see what positive change it brings to your life.
6. When you are ready, say this incantation three times: *"I'll succeed in this interview, luck is on my side, I have confidence in myself, for this job I have applied. I'll ace this interview, I'll blow them away, for my talents, abilities, and strengths will clearly be on display. So mote it be."*
7. Take the water from your simmer pot and add it to a hot bath. Take time to relax in the water and clear your mind as you continue to enjoy the aromas.

Spell for Workplace Harmony

Best time to practice: During a Waxing Moon, or when workplace issues arise

We spend a large proportion of our time in the place where we work, so its atmosphere is important. Use this spell to bring harmony to your place of work and into your work relationships, particularly if you're having issues in this environment.

INGREDIENTS
Amazonite (for harmony)
Smoky quartz (to absorb negative energy)
Clear quartz (for harmony and peace)

TOOLS
Cleansing tools
Circle casting tools (optional)
Piece of paper and a pen
1 light blue candle (for peace)
Candleholder
Knife

METHOD

1. Cleanse your tools, crystals, and space.
2. Ground yourself, and cast a circle, if it is part of your practice.
3. On the paper, write down the names of the people in your workplace who you work with directly and indirectly. Underline the names of those you are having issues with or those who have a negative impact and who prevent the workplace from being a harmonious place.
4. Fold the paper in half and then place the crystals on top of it.
5. Carve the rune Wunjo (see page 184) into the candle to represent peace and harmony.
6. Place the candle in a candleholder, light the candle, and place the holder on top of the paper.
7. As the candle burns, visualize the specific ways your workplace needs more peace and harmony.
8. Let the candle burn out and open your circle.
9. Take the crystals to work and place them on your desk, or in the area in which you work, to keep drawing peace and harmony toward that place.

Candle Spell to Get a Raise

Best time to practice: On a New Moon, or the night before you ask for a raise

If you're in a job where the rate of pay doesn't reflect your level of skill, work, and productivity, it's time to ask for a raise. A spell alone won't secure the increase in wages that you want—you also have to be proactive in your approach by asking for the raise you desire. This candle spell will support these actions and help you to have the confidence and communication skills to achieve it.

TOOLS
Cleansing tools
Circle casting tools (optional)
1 green candle (for money)
1 orange candle (for success)
1 yellow candle (for communication)
Knife
Lighter or matches

METHOD

1. Cleanse your tools and space.
2. Take some time to ground yourself, then cast a circle, if it is part of your practice.
3. On the night before you ask for a raise, hold the candles in your hands, and whisper your intentions to them. Take your time and talk about why you deserve a raise and how you plan to ask for it. If you have a new wage in mind, state the figure as you speak your intentions. Think about what you will say to your boss and the possible words you might use.
4. With the knife, carve the words, "I will get the raise I deserve," into each candle. If you have a figure in mind you want your pay increased by, you can also carve this into the wax.
5. Light the candles and say this incantation once to each candle: *"I love my work and I love what I do, now I need to be paid my worth and due. So mote it be."*
6. Focus on the candles as you keep thinking about your exact intentions.
7. Let the candles burn out and open your circle.

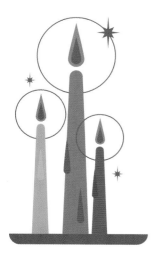

CHAPTER 6

Success, Happiness & Peace

Whether you're seeking inner peace, you want to manifest your dreams, or you want to attain the success you seek in any area of your life, you'll find the spell or ritual you've been looking for in this chapter. The magickal workings here are to help you manifest a successful, happy, and peaceful life.

Elemental Spell to Manifest Your Dreams

Best time to practice: On a New Moon

This candle spell calls upon the power of the four elements to help manifest your dreams. Fire is represented by the lit candles, bringing power to manifest your dreams. Earth is represented by the candle, symbolizing a stable foundation on which to manifest your dreams. Air is represented by the smoke from the candles and brings knowledge and the power of communication. Water is represented by the melting wax, bringing the power of transformation.

TOOLS
Cleansing tools
Circle casting tools (optional)
1 red or orange candle (to represent Fire)
1 green or brown candle (to represent Earth)
1 yellow or light blue candle (to represent Air)
1 dark blue or gray candle (to represent Water)
Piece of paper and a pen

METHOD

1. Cleanse your tools and space.

2. Start by grounding and centering your energies, then cast a circle, if it is part of your practice.

3. Place the 4 candles in a square on your altar or workspace, leaving plenty of room in the center.

4. Take some time to think about the dream you want to manifest. When you're ready, write about this dream in as much detail as you can. Remember to keep it realistic and achievable. Write about the ways in which you want or plan to achieve this dream and how your life will change when you manifest it into your life.

5. When you're ready, fold the paper three times toward you and place it in the center of the candles. Say this incantation: *"By the power of the elements four, the manifestation of my dream I do draw."*

6. Light the Fire candle and say: *"By the power of Fire, I manifest my dreams entire."*

7. Light the Earth candle and say: *"By the power of Earth, in my life my dreams are birthed."*

8. Light the Air candle and say: *"By the power of Air, to manifest my dreams I do prepare."*

9. Light the Water candle and say: *"By the power of Water, the realities of my dream get stronger. So mote it be."*

10. Focus on the paper in the middle of the candles and the dream you want to manifest to keep your intentions focused.

11. Let the candles burn out and open your circle.

12. Keep the paper on your altar or workspace until you have achieved your dream.

Inner Happiness Spell Jar

Best time to practice: During a Waxing Moon, or on a Full Moon

This spell jar will help to foster a deep sense of inner happiness, harmony, and peace within yourself.

INGREDIENTS
1 tsp dried lemon balm
(for happiness)
1 tsp dried hawthorn leaf (for
harmony and peace)
1 tsp honey or sugar (for feelings
of sweetness)
Citrine (for happiness and alignment)
Clear quartz (to remove
negative energy)
Tiger's eye (for harmony)

TOOLS
Cleansing tools
Circle casting tools (optional)
Jar with a lid
1 yellow candle (for happiness)

METHOD

1. Cleanse all your ingredients and tools.
2. Take a few moments to ground yourself. Cast your circle, if it is part of your practice.
3. Take your jar and add all the herbs and crystals. As you create your spell, say this incantation: *"Feelings of happiness this spell jar creates, it brings alignment and harmony, and all negative energies it negates. May the light of happiness shine from this jar of mine. So mote it be."*
4. Add a teaspoon of honey or sugar to sweeten your spell and say these words: *"This honey/sugar is to sweeten my spell, to bring happiness and harmony so all things are well. So mote it be."*
5. Take a yellow candle and light the wick, and then drop the hot wax around the lid of your jar to seal in your magick.
6. Open your circle.
7. Place the jar somewhere you can see it as a reminder of your magick and to keep you focused on cultivating happiness in your life. Shake it regularly to reinvigorate its energies.

Manifest Success Crystal Grid

Best time to practice: On a Full Moon

A crystal grid consists of crystals placed in a certain, often geometric, pattern in order to amplify their energies for a specific purpose. This crystal grid will help you to manifest success into your life. This success may come in different forms for everyone, but this grid will help to draw the kind of success you are looking for.

INGREDIENTS

Pyrite (to attract abundance)
Citrine (for success)
Amethyst (for manifestation)
Clear quartz (to amplify the energies of the other crystals)

TOOLS

Cleansing tools
Piece of paper and a pen
Scissors

METHOD

1. Cleanse your tools, crystals, and space.

2. Ground your energies.

3. On the paper, draw a triangle, a symbol of manifestation. Inside the triangle, write about the kind of success you want to attract, being as specific as you can.

4. Cut the triangle out with a pair of scissors and place it on a flat surface.

5. On the triangle, arrange the crystals in a Sun shape, so the crystals radiate outward from around the paper triangle in the center. You can also use other crystals that are specifically aligned with the success you want to achieve. See page 179 for crystals correspondence to help you choose.

6. As you create your crystal grid, you might like to say a mantra along the lines of, "*I manifest success,*" so you can keep your intentions focused.

7. Once you've finished creating your grid and you're happy with where all the crystals are placed, say these words: "*I manifest success into my life, I open the doors so the success I seek floods into my life. I manifest the success I desire and deserve. So mote it be.*"

8. To activate your grid, use your index finger to draw an invisible line between each crystal, to energetically connect them all, starting from the center and working your way outward. Do this simply by touching each crystal, one after the others.

9. Leave your grid out until you feel you have attained the success you desire.

Creativity Boosting Candle Spell

Best time to practice: On a New Moon or Wednesday

This spell is useful if you are looking to increase your creativity levels and bring a spark of inspiration. Whether you're working on a project at school or at work, or are just struggling for original ideas in any kind of situation, this spell will give you the boost of creativity you're looking for.

INGREDIENTS
1 tsp dried rosemary (to stimulate creativity)
1 tsp dried lavender (for relaxation, to allow creativity to flow)
1 bay leaf (to bring inspiration)

TOOLS
Cleansing tools
Circle casting tools (optional)
Mortar and pestle
A piece of paper
1 orange candle (for creativity)
1 tsp of base oil such as grapeseed or sunflower oil
Cauldron or heatproof dish
Lighter or matches

METHOD

1. Cleanse your tools and space.
2. Ground yourself, and cast a circle, if it is part of your practice.
3. Take the rosemary, lavender, and bay leaf and grind them up in a mortar and pestle to a rough powder.
4. Sprinkle the herb power in a thin layer onto the piece of paper.
5. Cover the orange candle in a thin layer of olive oil.
6. Roll the candle in the herb powder so it sticks to the oil, covering the candle in a thin layer of herbs.
7. Place the candle in a cauldron or heatproof dish and light the candle.
8. As the candle burns, say the words as you touch the relevant parts of your body.
Touch your eyes and say, *"May I see the things in life that inspire me."*
Touch your nose and say, *"May I smell things that enrich my thoughts."*
Touch your lips and say, *"May my mouth be ready to say 'yes' to new opportunities."*
Touch your ears and say, *"May I hear things that inspire creative thoughts and actions."*
Place your hands together and say, *"May my hands work creatively together. So mote it be."*
9. Let the candle burn for a few minutes as you visualize drawing the creativity you want toward you.
10. Blow out the candle and open your circle.
11. Light the candle again when you are in need of a creative boost.

Learning & Studying Success Candle Spell

Best time to practice: On a Full Moon or Wednesday

This spell is to help with studying and learning. Whether in or out of school, it will help to improve your memory, concentration, and focus so you can remember, recall, and understand a greater amount of information.

INGREDIENTS

1 tsp dried rosemary, ground (for memory)
1 tsp dried peppermint, ground (to increase alertness)
1 tsp dried lemon balm, ground (for focus)
1 tsp dried turmeric, ground (for concentration)
Citrine (for intelligence)
Black tourmaline (to improve memory)
Tiger's eye (to stimulate mental activity)

TOOLS

Cleansing tools
Circle casting tools (optional)
Piece of paper and a pen
1 orange candle (for learning)
Knife
Plate
Lighter or matches

METHOD

1. Cleanse your tools and ingredients.
2. Ground yourself, then cast a circle, if it is part of your practice.
3. In the middle of a piece of paper, write down exactly what you need help to learn. If you are taking an educational course or are at school, write down the name of the courses and subjects you want help with learning.
4. Take the knife and carve the rune Kaunan (see page 184), the rune of knowledge, into the wax.
5. Place the orange candle on the plate. To make it stand up, drip some hot wax onto the plate and place the candle onto it to hold it in place.
6. Sprinkle the dried herbs around the candle on the plate.
7. Place the crystals around the candle, on top of the herbs.
8. Light the candle and say this incantation: *"I wish to become wiser, I am a seeker of knowledge. I commit myself to learning as I move past any blockage. Help my concentration, aid my memory, this spell is my studying success remedy. So mote it be."*
9. Let the candle burn out then open your circle.
10. Keep the crystals nearby when you are studying or take them to school to help ensure learning success.

New Year Peace Spell

Best time to practice: New Year's Eve

This spell will help to welcome in peace, happiness, health,
and wealth into the new year.

INGREDIENTS

1 tsp dried chamomile,
ground (for peace)

1 tsp ground cinnamon
(for good luck)

1 tsp dried basil, ground (for wealth)

1 tsp ground cumin (for good health)

1 tsp dried lemon balm, ground
(for happiness)

Dragon's blood incense stick or
cone (to increase the potency of
your spell)

TOOLS

Cleansing tools

Lighter or matches

Circle casting tools (optional)

Incense holder

1 white candle (for peace)

A copy of the peace symbol

Knife

METHOD

1. Cleanse your tools, ingredients, and space with the dragon's blood incense, then let it burn throughout your spell in a holder.

2. Ground yourself, and then cast a circle, if it is part of your practice.

3. Place a large copy of the peace symbol (printed out or drawn) on a flat surface and, using it as a guide, sprinkle the herbs along the lines so they form the shape of the symbol.

4. On the white candle, carve the new year ahead in the wax. Also carve words such as "peace," "good luck," "wealth," "good health," and anything else you want from the new year.

5. When you've finished, place the candle in the middle of the peace symbol where the two lines intersect at the vertical line.

6. Light the candle and say: *"I welcome in the new year, may only peace enter here. May this new year bring all good things such as happiness, luck, and wealth, and may it bring abundant opportunities and may I enjoy good health. So mote it be."*

7. Let the candle burn out and open your circle.

8. Gather up the herbs and throw them into the wind to offer your spell to the universe.

Happy Pet Spell

Best time to practice: On a New Moon or Full Moon

This simple candle spell will help to surround your pet with positive energy and boost their feelings of happiness.

INGREDIENTS

½ tsp dried lemon balm, ground (for happiness)
½ tsp catnip (optional, for happiness, if the spell is for a cat)

TOOLS

Cleansing tools
Circle casting tools (optional)
1 yellow or white tea light (for happiness)
A pen
Your pet's collar (if they have one)
Lighter or matches

METHOD

1. Cleanse your tools, herbs, and space.
2. Ground yourself, and cast a circle, if it is part of your practice.
3. If you can get your pet to join you in your circle, do so, since it will help you to focus your energies, but don't worry if you can't.
4. Take the tea light and sprinkle the herbs on top of the candle. Light the candle. Using a pen, draw the Wunjo rune (see page 184), the rune for happiness and harmony, on the inside of your pet's collar, so they can take happiness wherever they go. Say these words as you do: *"May this spell bring a deep sense of happiness to (your pet's name). May it fill them with contentment and bliss, bringing them peace of mind that will follow them throughout their life, so any unhappiness will be dismissed. So mote it be."*
5. Take time to visualize a bright yellow light forming around your pet to represent feelings of happiness.
6. Let the candle burn out and open your circle.

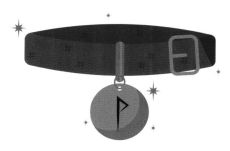

CHAPTER 7

Wish &
Good Luck Magick

Many people have cast a wish spell without even realizing it. When you blow out candles on a birthday cake, we are told to make a wish. This is one of the simplest forms of wish magick. The same can be said about wishing for good luck or doing certain things to stop bad luck attaching itself to you. This chapter contains a selection of all-purpose wish and good luck spells that can be used fulfill your desires, bring good fortune, and attract life-changing opportunities.

Knot Wish Spell

Best time to practice: During a Waxing Moon, or on a New Moon

Knot spells are an ancient form of folk magick. By the physical act of tying knots, you are securing your intentions into a length of cord (or anything that can be knotted) in order to cast your spell. Using knot magick, this spell will help to bring your wishes into reality.

TOOLS
Cleansing tools
Circle casting tools (optional)
A long piece of string or cord in the color associated with your wish (see color correspondence on page 180)

METHOD

1. Cleanse your tools and space.
2. Ground your energy, and cast a circle, if it is part of your practice.
3. Hold the cord in your hands, thinking about your wish.
4. Lay the cord vertically over your lap so that one end is on your knees and the other is dangling down toward the floor.
5. Starting at the furthest end of the cord that dangles down, so you are tying your knots toward you for attraction, begin tying the nine knots. For each knot, say the relevant part of the chant below:
"By knot number one, my spell has begun.
By knot number two, my wish will come true.
By knot number three, my wish I will see.
By knot number four, my wish grows more.
By knot number five, my wish is alive.
By knot number six, my wish is fixed.
By knot number seven, my wish will leaven.
By knot number eight, my wish I state.
By knot number nine, my wish is mine."
6. Cut off any excess cord remaining.
7. Open your circle.
8. Hang the cord where you spend a lot of time or in a place associated with your wish.

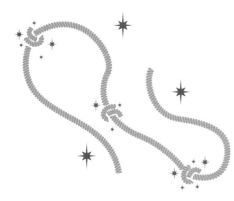

Wishing Well Jar Ritual

This ritual was adapted from Cassandra Eason's *1001 Spells*, No. 407. Throwing a coin into a wishing well is an ancient form of wish magick and is believed to draw good fortune. This ritual is particularly effective when performed at the beginning of a new period of time, in order to help manifest your wishes.

TOOLS

Cleansing tools
Large jar with a lid, filled with water
3 coins in your country's currency (preferably silver)

METHOD

1. Cleanse your tools and space.
2. Ground yourself, and cast a circle, if it is part of your practice.
3. Sit for a moment and think about the specific wish you want to make.
4. Hold the first coin in your hand, and say: "*Wishing well, wishing well, grant me my wish. Take this first coin and make my wish come true.*"
5. Drop the coin into the jar of water and make your wish.
6. Hold the second coin in your hand, and, thinking about your wish, say: "*Wishing well, wishing well, grant me my wish. Take this second coin and make my wish come true.*"
7. Drop the coin into the jar of water and repeat your wish.
8. Hold the third coin in your hand and say: "*Wishing well, wishing well, grant me my wish. Take this last coin and make my wish come true. So mote it be.*"
9. Drop the last coin into the jar of water and say your wish out loud.
10. Replace the lid on the jar. You can then place the jar to one side and use it as a wishing well again another time.
11. Open your circle.

Turn Your Luck Around Tarot Spell

This spell harnesses the energies of tarot cards to improve your luck.

INGREDIENTS

1 tsp dried basil (for good luck)
1 tsp ground cinnamon (for power)
Citrine (for prosperity)
Carnelian (for good fortune)

TOOLS

Cleansing tools
Circle casting tools (optional)
Tarot deck
Plate
Good luck symbols such as horshoes or four-leaf clovers

METHOD

1. Cleanse your tools and ingredients.
2. Ground yourself, and cast your circle, if it is part of your practice.
3. Place the following tarot cards in the middle of the plate, in a pile facing upward: the Wheel of Fortune (for turning luck around), The World (for fulfillment), Nine of Cups (for a wish come true), Ace of Pentacles (for luck), The Star (for hope and renewal).
4. Sprinkle the cards with the herbs and spices and then add the crystals on top.
5. Arrange symbols of good luck around the tarot cards.
6. When ready, hold your hand over the plate and say: "*I feel my luck change from today, I feel good luck coming my way. My unlucky streak is over, from this run of bad fortune I have closure. So mote it be.*"
7. Open your circle, leaving the tarot cards where you can see them, until the New Moon.

Wish Come True Spell

Best time to practice: On the New Moon or anytime you want to make a wish

Bay leaves are known as a "wishing herb" and are a simple but very efective way to incorporate wish magick into your practice. This spell will help you to focus your attentions on one specific wish, working at it to make it a reality.

INGREDIENTS
1 bay leaf

TOOLS
Cleansing tools
Circle casting tools (optional)
Pen
Lighter or matches
Cauldron or heatproof dish

METHOD

1. Cleanse your tools, ingredients, and space.
2. Take time to ground your energies, then cast a circle, if it is part of your practice.
3. Take a pen and, on the bay leaf, write one or two words that represent your wish.
4. Hold the bay leaf in your hand and speak your wish out loud as clearly as possible.
5. Using a lighter or matches, carefully burn the bay leaf over the cauldron or heatproof dish, saying: *"As this bay leaf burns, may it bring the wish I speak toward me as I wish it into reality. So mote it be."*
6. Drop the burning leaf into the cauldron or heatproof dish to burn.
7. Once it has all burned and turned to ash, open your circle.

Good Luck Lemon Cleanse Spell

Best time to practice: During the Waxing Moon, or on a New Moon or Thursday

Some people in life believe they are born unlucky or naturally attract misfortune, but this belief can act like a barrier, stopping them from attracting and receiving good luck in their life. This lemon spell will help to remove any mental or emotional blockages you may have that stand in the way of receiving good fortune, opening the door for luck and blessings.

INGREDIENTS
Half a lemon (to cleanse negative energies, allowing good luck to enter)
1 tsp dried rosemary, ground (to enhance luck)
1 tsp ground cinnamon (to heal blockages)

TOOLS
Cleansing tools
Circle casting tools (optional)
1 green candle (for good fortune)
Lighter or matches

METHOD

1. Cleanse your tools, ingredients, and space.
2. Ground your energy before you begin, then cast a circle, if it is part of your practice.
3. Sit the lemon half facing upward. In the flesh of the lemon, place a green candle so it stands upright.
4. Sprinkle the rosemary onto the lemon and around the candle, and light the wick.
5. Visualize the lemon cleansing away any negative energies that act as a blockage to good luck, watching these energies getting smaller until they are no more. When you're ready, say: "*All blockages to good fortune melt away, I receive the good luck that comes my way. These blockages are gone, they no longer hold me back, the road is cleared and now good luck I attract. So mote it be.*"
6. Let the candle burn out and open your circle.
7. Bury the lemon in your garden or somewhere near on your property. to keep the channels open to attract luck toward you.

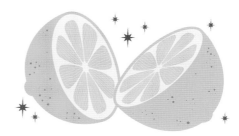

Whisker Wish Spell Bottle

Best time to practice: During a Waxing Moon or on a New Moon

Cat whiskers are considered both a good luck charm and a powerful ingredient in wish magick. This spell will help you to manifest any kind of wish by making sure luck is on your side. Any whisker used in your spells or rituals should be shed naturally and should NEVER be cut from your cat.

TOOLS
Cleansing tools
Circle casting tools (optional)
Piece of paper and a pen
Jar with lid
3 cat whiskers

METHOD

1. Cleanse your tools and space.
2. Ground your energy and cast a circle, if it is part of your practice.
3. On a small piece of paper (big enough to fit in your jar), write down your wish, being as specific as possible.
4. Roll the piece of paper up and put it in the bottle.
5. Hold one whisker and say these words:
"These whiskers I've collected will bring me good luck and fortune, they will help me to manifest my wish and make it come true. So mote it be."
6. Add the paper to the bottle.
7. Repeat the same words for the remaining whiskers, placing them in the bottle before securing the lid.
8. Open your circle.
9. Keep the bottle near you or in a space associated with the wish you have made. Shake it regularly to give your spell a boost of energy.

Banish Bad Luck Spell

Best time to practice: On the New Moon or anytime you want to make a wish

Sometimes, despite our best efforts to break away from bad luck, nothing seems to shift misfortune. The only way to change the situation is to banish the bad luck that follows you. This spell will help to banish any kind of bad fortune, and to restore balance in your life by using the number nine, which raises your vibrational frequencies so you can have control over your bad luck.

TOOLS

Cleansing tools
Circle casting tools (optional)
Cauldron or heatproof dish
Lighter or matches
Piece of paper and a pen

METHOD

1. Cleanse your tools and ingredients.
2. Ground your energy before you begin, then cast a circle, if it is part of your practice.
3. On a piece of paper, write the words "bad luck" nine times in a spiral shape, starting outward and moving inward as you write.
4. Next, across the spiral in nine vertical lines, write the words: "My bad luck is banished."
5. Turn over the paper, and on this side write a short letter about how this run of bad luck stops here, since it no longer has power over you. This is a petition of your intent.
6. Take the paper and tear it into nine pieces, then, using a lighter or matches, set the pieces alight before placing them in the cauldron or heatproof dish to burn.
7. As they burn, say this incantation nine times: *"As my petition burns, my bad luck is banished, my misfortunes do vanish. Bad luck is removed, my life is improved. Bad luck no longer has power over me. So mote it be."*
8. Let your petition burn completely and cool before disposing of the remains somewhere away from your home.
9. Open your circle.

CHAPTER 8

Protection

Protection spells are one of the most popular forms of magick. It's important that we know how to protect ourselves, whether that is energetically, physically, emotionally, or mentally. This chapter contains a range of different protection spells and rituals to bring you protection in all areas of life.

Protection Amulet Spell

Best time to practice: On a Full Moon or Saturday

Amulets are an ancient form of protection—they ward off danger and negative energy. They are traditionally made of natural materials such as crystals, metal, and even teeth, bones, and claws, but pieces of jewelry, can be worn as artificially made amulets, too. For it to offer protection, it must be an item you are willing to wear daily.

TOOLS
Cleansing tools
Circle casting tools (optional)
Item of jewelry

METHOD

1. Cleanse your tools and space.
2. Ground your energy and cast a circle, if it is part of your practice.
3. Tune in to your breath for a while to calm yourself. Focus on breathing in through your nose and out through your mouth. Lengthen the breath, inhaling and exhaling to the count of two and then the count of three.
4. When you feel calm and ready, rub your hands together to raise your energy for a few moments.
5. Hold your piece of jewelry in your hand and visualize the energy flowing from your hands into your amulet.
6. When ready, say these words: *"I create and bless this amulet for protection, may it guard against all negative energy, ill will and evil intent. May it keep me safe, wherever I go and shield me from any mental, physical, spiritual, and emotional harm. So mote it be."*
7. Open your circle.
8. Wear your amulet as often as possible for protection.

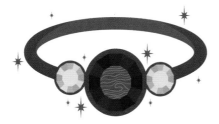

Protection Oil

Best time to practice: On a Full Moon

This multipurpose protection oil offers good all-round protection. You can also use it to anoint yourself, ritual items, and other spell ingredients, and to dress candles.

INGREDIENTS
1 tsp dried raspberry leaves, ground (brings protection to the user)
1 tsp ground black pepper (enhances protection spells)
1 tsp dried pine needles, chopped (to repel negativity)
1 tsp dried rosemary, ground (for energetic protection)
8 fl oz (250 ml) base oil such as grapeseed or sunflower oil

TOOLS
Cleansing tools
Bottle with a lid

METHOD

1. Cleanse your tools and ingredients.
2. Take a moment to ground yourself.
3. Place the raspberry leaves, black pepper, pine needles, and rosemary into your bottle.
4. Fill up the bottle with oil so there is twice as much oil in the bottle as there are herbs.
5. As you screw on the lid, say these words: *"May this oil give protection to all who use it. May it create a protective shield around me that repels everything that may do me harm. So mote it be."*
6. Leave the bottle in the moonlight for 3-4 hours to allow the Full Moon energies to charge up your oil.
7. After this time, it's ready to use. Use within 3 months.

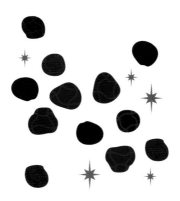

Freeze Out Protection Spell

This spell is a good way to protect yourself (or your friends and family) from any kind of harm or ill intent. It is used the block out the influence of the person who is a threat to you. To perform this spell, you must know the name of the person you wish to freeze out. The spell lasts as long as the paper is frozen in the ice. To reverse the spell, thaw the ice.

TOOLS
Cleansing tools
Circle casting tools (optional)
Piece of paper and a pen
Small bowl of water

METHOD

1. Cleanse your tools and space.
2. Ground your energy and cast a circle, if it is part of your practice.
3. On the paper, write the name of the person you want to freeze out.
4. Fold the paper away from you three times to symbolize a reduction in the person's influence.
5. Place the paper in the bowl of water until it's completely soaked then place the paper in your freezer. As you do, say: *"Freezer, freezer, cold as ice, I will no longer pay the price. Freeze out (name of person) influence, and keep it frozen continuous. This person is frozen out from my life and so is all their strife. So mote it be."*
6. Open your circle.
7. Keep the paper in the freezer for as long as you need to keep their influence or ill intent frozen out of your life.
8. When you feel the danger has passed and the person is no longer a threat, take the paper out of the freezer and allow it to thaw. As it thaws, say this incantation: *"You're no longer a danger to me, and because of this I set you free. So mote it be."*
9. Once it has thawed completely, you can throw the paper away.

Protective Black Salt

Do not use black salt outside—it will kill plant and insect life.

INGREDIENTS
A charcoal disc (to add color)
3 tsp salt (for protection)
2 tsp black pepper (for safety)
Cast iron flakes from a cauldron or cast iron cooking pan (for defense)

TOOLS
Cleansing tools
Mortar and pestle
Bottle or jar with lid

METHOD

1. Cleanse your tools, ingredients, and space.
2. Ground your energies.
3. In a mortar and pestle, grind down the charcoal disc into a powder and add it to your container. Then grind the herbs down and add them to the jar.
4. Add the salt and pepper along with any cast iron flakes from your cauldron or a cast iron pan from your kitchen.
5. Lid on, shake the container so the ingredients mix together. As you do, say these words: *"May this black salt bring me protection. May it protect me against any negative or unwanted energies and anything that seeks to do me harm. So mote it be."*
6. Your black salt is ready to use. It can be incorporated into any kind of protection spell.

Witch's Ladder of Protection Ritual

Best time to practice: On a New Moon, Full Moon, or Saturday

A Witch's ladder can be used for any purpose, including protection. It's a form of knot magick that includes charms and talismans related to the magick you want to make. This Witch's ladder is made to bring protection from any negative intent, and is inspired by Ella Harrison's *The Book of Spells*, page 53.

INGREDIENTS
3 pieces of black ribbon, string, wool, or cord, about 9 inches (25 cm) long
A piece of your hair (to bind the protection ladder to you)
9 items, such as bells, feathers, hag stones, crystals, and herbs of your choice, to weave into the ladder

TOOLS
Cleansing tools
Circle casting tools (optional)

METHOD

1. Cleanse your tools and space.
2. Ground your energy before you begin, then cast a circle, if it is part of your practice.
3. Take the three pieces of ribbon and knot them together at one end. As you do, set your intention. Think about the kind of protection you want this ladder to bring. Say the words: *"With knot one, the spell has begun."*
4. Start braiding the three cords together and, as you do, add the first item you've chosen to include in your ladder, keeping your intention at the forefront of your mind. Make a knot to secure the item.
5. Continue braiding, weaving in each item and making a knot to secure each one. Use these words with every subsequent knot you make:
"With knot two, protection I pursue.
With knot three, protection I see.
With knot four, the protection grows more.
With knot five, protection in my life arrives.
With knot six, this protection to me is fixed.
With knot seven, my protection is in accession.
With knot eight, protection I create.
With knot nine, with this protection I am aligned. So mote it be."
6. Open your circle.
7. Hang the ladder in your home or place it in your sacred space or altar area so it can draw protection toward you.

Empath Protection Tea

As empaths, we feel the emotions of others deeply. We take on their feelings as if they were our own, both in terms of positive and negative energies. For this we need to be able to protect our own energies so we don't feel drained or overwhelmed by the energies of others. Use this tea whenever you need it to create a protective shield that will protect your own personal energy.

INGREDIENTS
Kettle of hot water
1 tsp dried dandelion leaf, ground
(for releasing stored negativity)
1 tsp dried lavender, ground
(to remove negativity on a
spiritual level)
1 tsp dried lemon balm, ground
(to heal energetic wounds and
restore calm)
1 tsp dried rosemary, ground (to
help you understand the difference
between your emotions and the
emotions of others)
1 tsp dried yarrow, ground
(for protection from the emotions
of others)

TOOLS
Cleansing tools
Tea ball strainer
Mug

METHOD

1. Cleanse you ingredients, tools, and space.
2. Add the herbs to the tea ball strainer.
3. Fill a mug with hot water and then add the tea ball strainer so that the herbs can infuse the water. Leave to steep for 5–7 minutes.
4. As it's steeping, hold your dominant hand over the cup and say these words: *"May this tea create a shield around me to protect my energies. May it protect me from the emotions and feelings of others that drain me. May it help to heal energetic wounds left by others so I remain strong. Their energies no longer affect or hurt me. I am protected. So mote it be."*
5. Enjoy your tea. As you drink it, visualize an energetic force forming around you so the emotions and feelings of others bounce straight off it, and they can no longer reach and affect you.

Note: Rosemary should be avoided by people with epilepsy. All herbal teas must be taken with caution by anyone taking prescribed medication. Check with your medical herbalist or doctor before drinking this tea, and avoid if pregnant.

Binding Spell

Best time to practice: During a Waning Moon, or on a Full Moon

This is a powerful protection spell, which can be used on people or things, such as unhealthy habits or negative thinking. Use this spell with caution—it is not for binding an ex-love to you or stopping a lover from leaving you. It is only meant for when you have pursued other avenues to sort out an issue first. You must be incredibly specific with your intentions, to avoid possible unforeseen and unwanted outcomes.

INGREDIENTS
1 dried bay leaf, ground (to bind)
1 tsp dried rosemary, ground (for protection)
1 tsp dried nettle, ground (for boundary setting)

TOOLS
Cleansing tools
Circle casting tools (optional)
Piece of paper or a photo of the person or thing you want to bind (optional)
Pen
Length of black ribbon or string
Matches or a lighter
Heatproof dish

METHOD

1. Cleanse all your herbs, tools, and space.
2. Ground your energy before you begin, and cast a circle, if it is part of your practice.
3. Write the full name of the person or thing you wish to bind on a piece of paper, or on the back of a photo of the person or thing you wish to bind.
4. Take some time and visualize the person, thing, or situation in your mind and exactly why you are binding them. Once you're clear on your intentions, write them on the paper on the same side as the person or thing's name.
5. Place ground-up bay leaf, rosemary, and nettle into the center of the paper. Fold the paper or photo up so the herbs are safe inside.
6. Wrap a piece of black ribbon or string around the piece of paper or photo tightly. As you do, say: "*To be protected from all calamity and harm, I use this magick charm. With these words I bind thee, so you can now let me be. To be protected from all harm, I now seal this charm.*" When you've finished, place the paper or photo on the floor and stamp on it. As you do, say, "*So mote it be!*" in a loud voice.
7. Open your circle.
8. Keep the paper out of sight until a time when the danger has passed, when you want or need to unbind the person, thing, or situation.
9. To unbind, carefully and slowly remove the bindings, and say, "*I unbind you from the spell I cast, this binding now will no longer last. I release you from the effects of my charm, but I will continue to be kept safe from harm. The spell I cast has now been reversed and its effects on you have now dispersed. So mote it be.*"
10. Burn the paper in a heatproof dish and dispose of the ashes and herbs in the trash or give them back to the earth by burying them.

CHAPTER 9

Banishing, Releasing & Removing Magick

Banishing, removing, and releasing magick is used in all forms of Witchcraft. At its core, it involves making something go away, whether in the past, present, or future. This chapter focuses on spells and rituals that involve release, banishment, and removal of any kind of unwanted energy in many different forms. This could be the removal of curses and hexes, banishment of negative energy that may stop you moving forward in life, or the release of past hurts and negative thoughts.

Release The Past Spell

Best time to practice: During a Waning Moon

This spell can help to facilitate the release of different emotions, feelings, and any other unwanted energies from the past that no longer serve you or which are holding you back in life.

INGREDIENTS
A small piece of fruit or vegetable, a banana peel, or fallen leaves

TOOLS
Cleansing tools
Circle casting tools (optional)
Piece of paper and a pen
Length of string

METHOD

1. Cleanse your tools and ingredients.
2. Ground yourself and cast a circle, if it is part of your practice.
3. On a piece of paper, write the thing you want to release, being as specific as you can.
4. Take a piece of fruit or a vegetable, a few fallen leaves, or a banana peel, and, using a length of string, attach your piece of paper to it.
5. Bury it in the ground and say these words: *"I give this (name of item) back to the earth, I place this in the soil, as it decays and decomposes, I release of what with I toil. The past will no longer have hold over me, and from its effect I now am free. So mote it be."*
6. Open your circle.
7. As the item you've chosen decomposes, you will gradually release the energies or things you want to let go of.

Return-to-Sender Spell

Best time to practice: During a Waning Moon, or on a Full Moon

This powerful return-to-sender spell is great when you feel bad or if unwanted energies or malicious magick have been sent your way, or if you feel you've accumulated negative energies from others. It will return these unwanted energies to where they came from, thereby removing them, and their influences, from your life. Some Witches often call this kind of spell a karma spell.

INGREDIENTS
Black salt (see page 92) or white salt

TOOLS
Cleansing tools
Circle casting tools (optional)
1 black candle (for protection)
Lighter or matches
Piece of paper and a pen
A small photo of the person or people in question (optional)
Small compact with two mirrors inside (to reflect negative energy back to the sender)

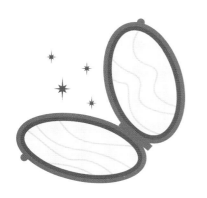

METHOD

1. Cleanse your tools, ingredients, and space. Don't catch your own reflection in the mirrors until after you've cleansed them during the spell.
2. Ground your energies and cast a circle, if it is part of your practice.
3. Around the candle, make a circle of black salt big enough to fit the compact inside later on in the spell. The black salt will offer protection from such energies in the future and will help to remove the negative or unwanted energies.
4. Light the candle for protection as you cast this spell.
5. On a small piece of paper, write, "I send back the negative energy (name) sent me, I return it to its sender." Open the mirror. If you don't know their names, you can visualize the person and then project that into the mirror by focusing on it as you think about them. You can also use a small photo of the person or people in question if you have them. If it's to return general negative energy from multiple sources, write something like, "I return all the energy that I have accumulated from others back to where it came from."
6. Fold up the paper and put it between the two mirrors, then close up the compact, making sure you don't catch your own reflection in it while you're doing so.
7. Put the compact in the circle of black salt until the candle has nearly burned out. Extinguish the candle as a symbol of the removal of these unwanted energies, returning them to their senders.
8. Open your circle.
9. Keep the compact closed and out of sight until you feel that all the negative energy has completely returned to where it came from.
10. Open the compact and cleanse it before using again, and burn the piece of paper or photo inside.

Spell Jar to Remove Bad Attitudes

Best time to practice: During a Waning Moon, or on a New Moon or Full Moon

If there is someone in your life with a bad attitude, who is affecting you in any kind of negative way, this spell jar will help to remove these bad attitudes, replacing them with peaceful and positive energies.

INGREDIENTS
6 drops of vinegar (to stop bad attitudes returning)
1 tsp dried salt, ground (to cleanse the bad attitudes)
1 tsp dried rosemary, ground (for a fresh start)
1 tsp dried cedar needles, ground (to clear negative emotions)
1 tsp dried chamomile, ground (to bring peaceful energies)
1 tsp ground cinnamon (to enhance the power of your spell)

TOOLS
Cleansing tools
Circle casting tools (optional)
Pocket-sized jar with lid
Piece of paper and a pen
Lighter or matches
1 black candle (for removal and protection)

METHOD

1. Cleanse your tools, ingredients, and space.
2. Ground yourself and cast a circle, if it is part of your practice.
3. Add all the dried ingredients to the jar.
4. On a piece of paper, write: "I remove the bad attitudes of (full name of person)."
5. Fold the paper away from you three times to symbolize removal. As you do, visualize the person you wish to remove the bad attitudes from and think of how it will affect you and your life when these attitudes have gone.
6. Place the paper in your jar on top of the dried ingredients.
7. Take the vinegar and, before you add it to the jar, say these words:
 "I remove the bad attitudes from (name of person), they are no longer around to affect me. Bad attitudes be gone! I remove them from thee. They are gone from the present time, and the future too. Their bad attitudes will not return to have a negative impact on me. So mote it be."
8. Add the drops of vinegar to the jar on top of the folded piece of paper.
9. Make sure the lid is secured and, using a lit black candle, drop hot wax around the lid to seal it.
10. Open your circle.
11. Put the jar in your pocket when you interact with the person in question. The more the person is exposed to the magickal energies of the jar, the more their bad attitudes will be removed.

Banishing Powder

Best time to practice: During a Waning Moon

This potent banishing powder can be used as part of a banishing spell or on its own. A little goes along way!

INGREDIENTS
1 tsp black pepper, ground
(to remove negative energy)
1 tsp cayenne pepper, ground
(to remove obstacles)
1 tsp cinnamon, ground
(to boost energy)
1 tsp sea salt (for banishing)
1 tsp bay leaves, chopped
(for elimination)

TOOLS
Cleansing tools
Jar with a lid
Knife
Spoon

METHOD

1. Cleanse your tools and ingredients.
2. Ground your energies.
3. Take a jar and add all the powdered herbs and spices.
4. Take a spoon and stir up the mixture in a counter-clockwise direction to represent removal.
5. Say these words: *"May this powder banish those things from my life that no longer serve me. Whether an emotion, feeling, or person, may they be removed far away from me. So mote it be."*
6. This powder can be used to anoint candles, or can be sprinkled on the belongings of the person you want to banish. It can also be sprinkled at the threshold of your home so the person you wish to banish has to walk through it. It can also be added to olive oil to make a banishing oil.

Simmer Pot to Remove Grief & Heartache

Best time to practice: During a Waning Moon, or on a New Moon or Full Moon

Grief and heartache are a part of life. At some point, we all go through situations that cause us to grieve the loss of people, things, or the past. In the same way, we all experience heartache. This simmer pot is here to reduce and manage these overwhelming feelings.

INGREDIENTS

1 sliced-up lemon (to cleanse)
2 tbsp fresh or dried lavender (for calm and peace)
2 tbsp fresh or dried marjoram (to bring emotional healing)
1 tbsp rowan berries (for emotional resilience and healing the heart)
Handful of fresh or dried rose petals (to gently heal grief)
Water
1 bay leaf

TOOLS

Cleansing tools
Medium-sized pan

METHOD

1. Cleanse your ingredients, tools, and workspace.
2. Place all your ingredients except the bay leaf into the pan, then add enough water so all the ingredients are floating.
3. On the bay leaf, write, "remove heartache," on one side and, "remove grief," on the other side. Add this to the pan.
4. Put the pan on the stove on a low heat and simmer for 2–3 hours to let the aromas infuse your kitchen and home.
5. After 2 hours, stand next to the pan. Take some deep breaths as you breath in the fragrances coming from the simmer pot. Visualize the aromas as a white light surrounding you, bringing your heart healing, to help you let go of your grief and heartache.
6. Hold your hands over the pot and imagine all your grief and heartache flowing into the simmer pot. If you get emotional, let it go rather than holding it in. Don't be afraid to cry and let your feelings out, so that your emotions flow freely in a way that feels right to you. When you feel ready, say these words as many times as feels right, as you continue to visualize your grief and heartache pouring into the water: *"Grief be gone, let my heartache heal, let these things be removed from my life so I can heal from this ordeal. So mote it be."*
7. When you've finished, let the water cool. Throw the herbs and spices away and find a place somewhere away from your home to return the liquid back to the earth, to symbolize removal.

Cutting the Cord Ritual

This spell is used to sever the ties you have with a person (like an ex-partner after a breakup), a relationship (platonic or romantic), a place, state of mind, or something that no longer serves you, like an addiction. It is used like an energetic cleanse that helps to separate you from toxic attachments in your life.

TOOLS
Cleansing tools
Circle casting tools (optional)
Knife
2 black candles (for protection)
4 in (10 cm) red string or wool
(to represent the bond you are
about to cut)
Lighter or matches
Plate
Scissors

METHOD

1. Start by cleansing all your tools, ingredients, and space.
2. Ground your energy and cast a circle, if it is part of your practice. Casting a circle may help to give you more protection against the emotions associated with cutting the cord.
3. Use the knife to carve your full name into one candle and, on the other candle, carve the full name of the person or thing you want to part from.
4. Use a piece of red string or wool and tie one end to one candle (about half way down) and tie the other end of the string to the other candle.
5. Stand the candles far enough away from each other on the plate that the string is tight in between. To make the candles stand up, light one of the candles and drip some candle wax onto the plate, then stand the candle in the melted wax.
6. Light the other candle and say this incantation: "*These candles are joined together by a bond, but the flame of one consumes the other. Today/ tonight, I say no more. I will no longer suffer or hurt because of (name). I will no longer let them have power over me. Today/tonight I take back that power. I sever the ties we share, I cut the cord between us. So mote it be.*"
7. You can either cut the string between the candles with scissors or you can let the candles burn down so the flames break the string in two. Go with the method that speaks to you and feels right to your practice.
8. Leave the candles to burn out and then open your circle.
9. Dispose of the wax and string from each candle in a separate place. Do not dispose of them together. This further symbolizes the cutting of the cord between you.

Magickal Tool Lemon Cleanse

Best time to practice: During the Waning Moon, or on a Full Moon

The tools used in magickal workings—such as a cauldron, knife, and athame—need to be regularly cleansed to remove any unwanted energies they may have picked up. This simple lemon cleanse is perfect for removing any kind of negative or unwanted energy that may accumulate over time and which may affect the outcome of your spells and rituals.

INGREDIENTS
The peel of 3 lemons (for cleansing)
12 fl oz (340 ml) warm water

TOOLS
Cleansing tools
Knife
Bowl
Spray bottle

METHOD

1. Fill the bowl with the warm water.
2. Place the lemon peel into the water. You can also add some lemon juice to the water for a deep cleanse.
3. Leave the peel to soak for at least 2 hours.
4. Remove the peel and put the lemon water into a spray bottle and use it to wash your magickal tools to remove any unwanted energy. Simply spray as much as you need, then wipe away. For a deep cleanse, wash the tools in the lemon water in the bowl and dry them afterward.

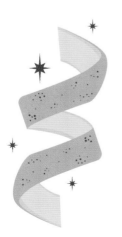

Release Mixture

Best time to practice: On a Full Moon

This mixture can be used in spells and rituals related to the releasing of old and unwanted energies to make way for new energies. It can be used in pouches, ritual baths, or charm bags, burned as incense on a charcoal disc, or used to dress candles when mixed with a tiny amount of oil.

iNGREDIENTS

1 tsp salt (to cleanse you of what no longer serves you)
2 tsp dried lavender (for peaceful energies)
2 tsp dried rose petals (for gentle release and healing)
2 tsp peppercorns (to banish negative vibrations)
1 tsp dried mint (to bring positive energy)
Little chips of amethyst (to release the past)
Smoky quartz (for letting go of the past)

TOOLS

Cleansing tools
Jar with a lid
Knife

METHOD

1. Cleanse your ingredients, tools, and space.
2. Ground your energies.
3. Add the flowers, herbs, spices, and crystals to your jar.
4. To focus on your intentions, hold out cupped hands and visualize holding a ball of black or gray light. This represents old and unwanted energies that no longer serve you. When you're ready, open your hands and visualize yourself releasing the energy so it can float away from you until it can't be seen or felt.
5. Using a knife, stir the ingredients in the jar in a counter-clockwise direction to symbolize release. As you do, say these words: *"May this mixture bring release to all areas and situations where it is needed, whether that be mental, emotional, spiritual, or physical energies. So mote it be."*
6. Place the jar in the light of the Full Moon (or under the Full Moon's energies if there is no moonlight) to charge for 2–3 hours. Then your release mixture is ready to use.

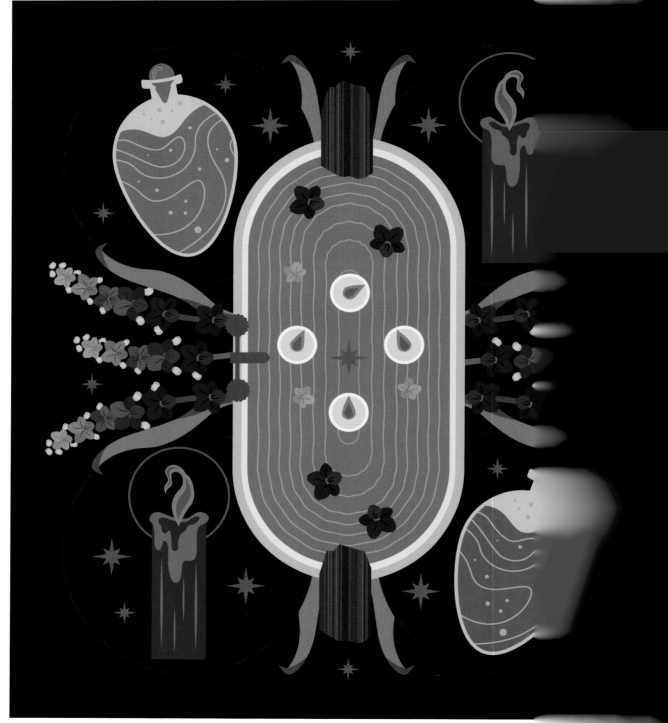

CHAPTER 10

Health, Well-being & Healing

Good physical, mental, and emotional health is integral to our sense of well-being. This collection of spells, rituals, recipes, and meditations will help to support good health and bring healing to where it's needed.

Good Health Tea Light Spell

Best time to practice: During a Waxing Moon, or on a Full Moon, New Moon, or a Sunday

This simple spell will help to attract good health.

TOOLS
Cleansing tools
1 white tea light (for good health)
Piece of paper and a pen
Lighter or matches

METHOD

1. Cleanse your tools and ingredients.
2. Ground your energy before you begin, then cast a circle, if it is part of your practice.
3. Take a piece of paper and, using the method on page 20 (or any method that feels right to use), make a sigil to signify good health. Use words to create your sigil such as, "I attract good health," or other words that feel right to you.
4. Take the tea light and remove the wax from the metal casing. Copy your sigil onto a small piece of paper, fold it up, and place it in the bottom of the metal case.
5. Place the wax back into the case on top of your sigil and light the wick. Say these words: *"Good health I attract, good health I draw toward me, as this candle burns, it brings me well-being and vitality. So mote it be."*
6. Let the candle burn out, and open your circle. Once the candle has burned out, there will be the paper left at the bottom. Once the remnants have cooled, carefully fold the metal of the tea-light case inward to cover the paper with your sigil drawn on it. Keep it on your altar, in a room where you spend most of your time, or even carry it with you to keep attracting good health toward you.

Preventing Nightmares Crystal Pouch

Best time to practice: During a Waning Moon, or on a Full Moon

Everyone has nightmares at one time or another. Some of us, however, have reoccurring nightmares and find it hard to control them, which can have a negative impact on our sense of well-being. These crystals will help to prevent nightmares as you sleep, stopping them from returning.

INGREDIENTS
Amethyst (to induce a peaceful sleep)
Dalmatian jasper (to remove negative thoughts)
Black obsidian (for protection against nightmares)
Hematite (to release any toxic energies before sleep)

TOOLS
Cleansing tools
Circle casting tools (optional)
Black fabric pouch with a tie

METHOD

1. Cleanse your tools, crystals, and space.
2. Ground your energies and cast a circle if it is a part of your practice.
3. Add all the crystals to the pouch, tying it securely so they can't fall out. As you do, say these words: *"May this pouch stop my nightmares and banish my bad dreams. May it prevent my nightmares from returning, helping me to have a peaceful night's sleep. So mote it be."*
4. Open your circle.
5. Once made, put the pouch under your pillow or at your bedside to prevent nightmares.
6. Cleanse the crystals regularly to stop any negativity from your nightmares attaching to them, keeping them working at their best.

Abracadabra Healing Amulet

Abracadabra is a common magick word. Although we may have heard the word on television, it is actually a powerful spell used for centuries to ward off fever or infection and to attract good health. It was believed that once a person put the amulet on their person, their illness would reduce. The pouch was traditionally worn around the neck, but placing it somewhere such as in your pocket or even in your bra (if you wear one) are good alternatives, just as long as it's on your person somehow.

TOOLS
Cleansing tools
Piece of paper and a pen
Fabric pouch with a tie

<u>METHOD</u>

1. Cleanse your tools and space.
2. Ground yourself before you begin, and cast a circle, if it is part of your practice.
3. On the top of a piece of paper, write the word ABRACADABRA.
4. On the line directly under the word, write the word again, but omit the last letter.
5. Repeat this process, writing the word ABRACADABRA again and again, dropping the last letter until you are left with just the letter "A" to make a triangle shape. This is to symbolize the reduction of illness and the increase in better health.
6. Cut out the triangle, place it in the pouch, and keep it on you.

```
ABRACADABRA
ABRACADABR
ABRACADAB
ABRACADA
ABRACAD
ABRACA
ABRAC
ABRA
ABR
AB
A
```

Inner Balance Candle Spell

In the modern world, it can be difficult to find a sense of balance. This candle spell will help you to achieve an inner sense of equilibrium and bring more balance into the areas of your life you most need it.

TOOLS
Cleansing tools
Circle casting tools (optional)
1 black candle (for shadow)
1 white candle (for light)
Lighter or matches
2 candleholders
2 pieces of paper and a pen
Cauldron or heatproof dish

<u>METHOD</u>

1. Cleanse your tools and workspace.
2. Ground your energy. Cast a circle, if it's part of your practice.
3. Place the candles in the two candleholders and light the wicks.
4. Sit and meditate on the areas of your life that need more balance.
5. On one piece of paper, write those things in your life you want to cultivate more of. This could be something such as peace, love, or happiness.
6. Burn the paper in the flame of the white candle, and say: *"May I cultivate inner balance in my life and attract the things in life I want more of."*
7. Put the flaming paper in the cauldron or heatproof dish to burn away.
8. On the other piece of paper write those things in your life you want less of, such as fear or depression.
9. Burn the paper in the flame of the black candle, and say: *"May I cultivate inner balance in my life and release those things I want less of in my life."*
10. Add the burning paper to the cauldron or heatproof dish.
11. Let the candles and paper burn out, and open your circle.

Bath Soak Ritual to Reduce Anxiety

Best time to practice: On a New Moon, or anytime you feel anxious

This bath soak is one of my favorite go-to rituals when I'm feeling anxious. The whole process of bathing, along with the purposely chosen crystals and herbs, is a relaxing experience, so take as much time as you need.

INGREDIENTS

2 tbsp dried or fresh chamomile (for calm)
2 tsp dried or fresh lavender (to reduce anxiety and bring peace)
Rose quartz (for emotional healing)
Amethyst (to soothe anxiety)
Clear quartz (for healing)
5 oz (or 150 g) Himalayan salt or Epsom salts

TOOLS

Cleansing tools
Muslin pouch

METHOD

1. Run a hot bath and pour the Himalayan salt or Epsom salts into the water.
2. Place the chamomile, lavender, and crystals in the pouch and add this to your bath and let their energy infuse your bath.
3. Climb into the bath and get comfortable. Close your eyes and breathe deeply in through your nose and out through your mouth. Take in the aromas and allow them to help reduce your anxiety and promote calm. Pour water over your body to allow the water to wash away your anxieties.
4. When you're ready, say these words three times: *"I am calm, I am peace, my anxiety now I do so release. So mote it be."*
5. Enjoy your bath for as long as you want. You could also put on some music that helps you to relax and bring peace as you enjoy your bath.
6. After your bath, keep the crystals with you to reduce your anxieties.

Tea Magick for Calm

Best time to practice: Anytime you need to foster a sense of calm

If you're feeling stressed, tense, and anxious, this tea will help to foster a sense of calm. I love tea recipes because they're an easy way to bring a little bit of magick into your daily routine.

INGREDIENTS
3 tsp dried lavender, ground (for peace)
3 tsp dried chamomile, ground (for calm)
3 tsp dried lemon balm, ground (to reduce anxiety)
3 tsp dried valerian, ground (to promote calm)
Kettle of hot water

TOOLS
Tea ball strainer
Mug

METHOD

1. Cleanse the ingredients, tools, and your space before you begin.
2. Ground your energies.
3. Place all the dried herbs into a jar or other kind of airtight container and mix well.
4. To make the tea, place the mixed herbs into a tea ball strainer.
5. Pour hot (but not boiling) water into your mug and place the tea ball strainer in the water.
6. Let the tea steep for 5–7 minutes.
7. Before you take your first sip, stir the tea in a clockwise direction to increase your sense of peace. As you do, say this simple incantation: "*May calmness be mine as I drink this tea, with every sip may it reduce my anxiety. If I'm holding on to any stress and tension, it will send calm in my direction. So mote it be.*"
8. Take your time and enjoy your tea, visualizing that with every sip, you become more calm.

Note: In rare cases, valerian can act as stimulant rather than a relaxant. As with all herbal teas, pay attention to any effects upon drinking. All herbal teas must be taken with caution by anyone taking prescribed medication. Check with your medical herbalist or doctor before drinking this tea, and avoid if pregnant.

Distance Healing Spell

Best time to practice: During a Waxing Moon, or on a New Moon or Full Moon

When we want to cast a healing spell for someone else, it's not always possible for that person to be with us at the time we make our magick—whether they live in another town, state, or even a different country. This spell can be used to bring healing energy to anyone who can't be physically with you at the time you cast it.

INGREDIENTS

Palo santo incense stick
(for cleansing)
1 tsp dried rosemary
(to stimulate immunity)
1 tsp dried lavender
(for emotional healing)
1 tsp dried cilantro
(to bring all-round healing)
3 pieces of clear quartz (for healing)
Photograph of the person you want
to heal, or the name of the person
written on a piece of paper

TOOLS

Cleansing tools
Incense holder
Circle casting tools (optional)
3 white candles (for purity)
Lighter or matches

METHOD

1. Cleanse your tools, ingredients, and space with the palo santo incense stick. Place the incense in an incense holder.
2. Ground your energies and cast a circle, if it is part of your practice.
3. Take the 3 white candles and arrange them in a triangle shape. In between each candle, place a piece of clear quartz. The shape of the triangle will help to manifest healing.
4. In the middle of the triangle, place the photo of the person you want to heal. If you don't have a photo, use a piece of paper with the full name of the person written on it.
5. Sprinkle the herbs on top of the photo or piece of paper and light the candles.
6. Say these words: *"Across the miles, this spell I cast, to bring healing energy to (name of person) that will last. Healing powers across the miles I do send, may it surround and comfort them so these energies can help mend. So mote it be."*
7. Let the candles burn out and dispose of the wax in the trash.
8. Leave the photo and herbs in the middle of the clear quartz triangle for as long as the person is in need of healing energies.

CHAPTER 11

Self-Love & Self-Care

Self-care and self-love is how we care for ourselves and our needs. It's not selfish or indulgent, it's essential for our well-being. Self-care is the way we can deal with the stresses of life as we take conscious steps to tend for our physical, emotional, and mental health in the long-term. Anything that is good for you and makes you feel better (but doesn't hurt anyone) can be classed as self-care, whether it's making sure you get enough sleep, eating healthily, having a relaxing bath, or confronting your shadows. The spells and rituals in this chapter are here to enrich your own self-care practices and bring more self-love into your life.

Self-Forgiveness Spell

Best time to practice: During a Waning Moon, on a Full Moon, or anytime you need self-forgiveness

We've all done things wrong in life—we're all human. When we do something wrong to ourselves, it can be very hard to forgive and we can carry around negative emotions—guilt, frustration, perhaps anger—that weigh us down. This spell will help the healing process of self-forgiveness, allowing you to let go of all these feelings and emotions, and bring inner peace and calm.

INGREDIENTS
1 apple (for healing)
1 tsp dried pine needles (to cleanse away the issue you are seeking self-forgiveness for)
1 tsp dried lavender, ground (for peace)
1 tsp dried rosemary, ground (for self-forgiveness)
1 tsp dried rose petals (to open the heart to self-forgiveness)

TOOLS
Cleansing tools
Circle casting tools (optional)
Piece of paper and a pen
Knife

METHOD

1. Cleanse your tools and ingredients.
2. Ground your energies and cast a circle, if it is part of your practice.
3. Sit and think about the issue you need help with. On a small piece of paper, write about what you want self-forgiveness for. Write it in the present tense, starting with the words "I forgive myself for. . . ." to help attract self-forgiveness toward you.
4. Cut the top off the apple about a third of the way down. Put the top to one side and hollow the other two-thirds of the apple out enough to fit the herbs and folded paper inside.
5. Place the herbs and your piece of paper inside the apple and put the top back on. As you do, say: "*Self-forgiveness I attract, any guilt, shame, and anger I subtract. I welcome in healing to lighten the load on my emotions and feelings. I let the things I did to myself go, they no longer have power over me. I forgive myself for what I did, I pardon myself, now I'm free. So mote it be.*"
6. Open your circle.
7. Bury the apple in your garden or an outdoor space. As the apple and herbs begin to rot, it will help to bring a sense of self-forgiveness and peace about the issue you are seeking forgiveness for.

Self-Love Spell Jar

Best time to practice: On a New Moon, Full Moon, or Friday

We all deserve to love ourselves and have confidence in who we are, but in our busy lives, we can often fall out of the habit of making time to cultivate this self-love in our lives. This spell jar will not only help you to focus on and attract self-love into all parts of your life but it will also give you a boost of confidence in yourself and who you are.

INGREDIENTS
Citrine (for self-confidence)
Tiger's eye (to keep you focused on cultivating self-love)
1 tsp dried peppermint (to attract self-love)
1 tsp dried rose petals (to evoke self-love)

TOOLS
Cleansing tools
Circle casting tools (optional)
Jar with a lid
1 pink candle (for self-love)

METHOD

1. Cleanse your tools, ingredients, and space.
2. Ground your energies first and cast a circle, if it is part of your practice.
3. Take a few minutes to meditate on the self-love you want to bring into your life. Visualize attracting this self-love and how it makes you feel. Take time to feel the energy of this love.
4. When you're ready, place the crystals inside the jar, followed by the peppermint and rose petals. While you do, focus on the feelings of self-love you cultivated at the beginning of the spell.
5. Put the lid on the jar, then hold the jar in your hands. Say the words: *"Self-love, self-love, come to me, I welcome it into my life today. I have confidence in the person I am and love the person I've become. I attract the love I know I need, I cultivate it each day and watch it grow, and in every part of my life, this self-love will overflow. So mote it be."*
6. Light the pink candle and drop hot wax around the lid of the jar to completely seal it.
7. Open your circle.
8. Place the jar somewhere you can see it regularly such as in the room you spend the most time in. To energize your spell jar, give it a regular shake.

Shadow Work Oil

Best time to practice: On a New Moon

Shadow work is the process of exploring the hidden and uncomfortable parts of ourselves that have a negative impact on our lives in the present. It means confronting personal traumas but doing this work is essential in order to understand who we truly are. It also helps to bring deep and lasting healing to the areas of life where it's needed. Working with your shadow self is not easy but this oil will help to support you during any kind of shadow work.

INGREDIENTS
4 tsp dried rosemary (for healing)
4 tsp black tea (for introspection)
4 tsp dried rose petals (for self-compassion and love)
4 tsp dried nettle (to move stagnant energy that stands in the way of healing)
12 fl oz (350 ml) base oil such as grapeseed or sunflower oil

TOOLS
Large jar with a lid

METHOD

1. Cleanse you tools, ingredients, and space.
2. Take a few moments to ground and center you energies before you start.
3. Add 2 teaspoons of each herb and flower to your jar and fill it up with oil so there is three times the amount of oil in the jar compared with the volume of the herbs. Place in a cool, dark place for a month. Shake the jar once a day.
4. After a month, strain the herbs away from the oil, then add another 2 teaspoons of each of the herbs to the oil that is left. Leave this in a cool dry place for another month to make a super concentrated oil.
5. After another month, strain the herbs away from the oil. As you do, say these words: *"May this oil support my shadow work. May it bring healing, self-compassion, and protection as I face my uncomfortable truths and shadows. May it help my time of introspection and move any stagnant energies that stand in the way of self-understanding and deep healing. So mote it be."*
6. Now your oil is ready to use, either to anoint yourself or to pair with candles that will be used in shadow work spells and rituals.

Note: Rosemary should be avoided by people with epilepsy.

Shadow Work Ritual

Best time to practice: On a New Moon or Wednesday

Shadow work is about being in a relationship with all parts of yourself, even the darker parts, and is a very powerful act of self-love and care in order to bring lasting healing into your life. Journaling is a good method to help you explore your shadows, and pulling a tarot card for each prompt can add another layer of understanding about what your shadows are and how you can heal them.

INGREDIENTS
Shadow work or winter oil (page 118 and page 45)

TOOLS
Cleansing tools
Circle casting tools (optional)
Piece of paper (or a notebook just for shadow work) and a pen
Tarot deck

METHOD

1. Cleanse you space and tools.
2. Ground your energies, then cast a circle, if it is part of your practice.
3. Anoint your pulse points with the shadow work or winter oil in order to support you during this ritual.
4. Take each of the prompts below in turn and write about them as fully and as honestly as you can in your shadow work journal. For each of the prompts, pull a tarot card (or as many as you feel you need to pull) for more insight. Write about the cards you pull and how they relate to you and the question. Remember to take your time. Shadow work is incredibly difficult but also incredibly important to your journey of self-discovery. Don't feel you have to do all the prompts at once. This is a ritual you can keep coming back to regularly over time, since shadow work can be exhausting.

SHADOW WORK PROMPTS

• Which emotions make you feel uncomfortable? Why do you think that is?
• Which emotions do you avoid? Why? How do you react when these emotions play out in your life?
• How do you cope with difficult emotions? List any unhealthy coping mechanisms that are hurting you. Why have you come to rely on these coping strategies?
• What parts of yourself do you judge? Why do you judge them? How do you judge others?
• What do you fear? How do these fears affect you? Why do you fear them? How do these fears change your behaviors and actions?

Love Myself More Elixir

Best time to practice: Anytime you need a little support

Crystal elixirs are made from fresh water and (very importantly) water-safe crystals. They can be used to heal and cleanse our bodies as well as bring in positive energy. This elixir, made from rose, smoky, and clear quartz, will help to foster feelings of self-love by removing any negative thoughts you might have about yourself and replacing them with feelings of self-compassion, patience, and self-love.

INGREDIENTS
Rose quartz (for self-love)
Clear quartz (for manifestation)
Smoky quartz (to transform negative energies into positive energies)
Drinking water

TOOLS
Cleansing tools
Circle casting tools (optional)
Jug

METHOD

1. Cleanse your tools, space, and ingredients.
2. Ground and center you energy, then cast a circle, if it is part of your practice.
3. Hold the rose quartz in your hand so you can feel its energy. Place it in the jug, and say: "*May this rose quartz bring self-love into my life.*"
4. Hold the smoky quartz in your hand so you can feel its energy. Place it in the jug, and say: "*May this smoky quartz transform any negativity into positive energy so there are no unwanted energies standing in the way of me loving myself wholly.*"
5. Hold the clear quartz in your hand so you can feel its energy. Place it in the jug, and say: "*May this clear quartz amplify the energies of the other crystals and help me manifest more self-love into my life.*"
6. Fill up the jug with water. Cover the jug wth a cloth and place it either in the light or under the energies of the Full Moon to charge for 2–3 hours; or, if you prefer, place it in the Sun for a few hours. Leave it to rest for 24 hours to allow the crystals to infuse the water.
7. When your elixir has been charged and rested, stir the elixir with your index finger in a clockwise direction for attraction, and repeat these words: "*As I drink this elixir, I welcome the powers of self-love into my life. May it remove any kind of doubt, I am worthy of this love both in and out. As above, so it is below, let the power of self-love around me grow. So mote it be.*"
8. If you plan to consume it straight away, sip your elixir throughout the day to open the doors of self-love.
9. Open your circle.

Inner Beauty Glamor Magick

Best time to practice: Every day or anytime you need a beauty boost

Glamor magick is about choosing something to wear or use such as make-up, cosmetic products, jewelry, or clothing, with intent, to enhance your natural beauty. It can't change your physical appearance but it can give you a boost of confidence in the way you look. This glamor ritual takes a daily activity and turns it into a magickal ritual you can use whenever you feel the need to bring your natural inner and outer beauty to the forefront and feel good about yourself.

TOOLS
Face wash
Facial moisturizer (optional)

METHOD

1. Ground your energies.

2. In the morning, before you start your day, splash your face with water. Visualize all negative and unwanted feelings and thoughts about your inner and outer beauty being washed away, so they won't interfere with the intent of this ritual.

3. Take your face wash and place the amount of product you usually use into your hand.

4. Place your other hand over the face wash. Visualize how you will feel when you have more confidence in yourself and in your inner and outer beauty.

5. Rub your hands together so the face wash is spread evenly between both hands.

6. Close your eyes and then gently wash around the eye area and say: *"May people see my true inner and outer beauty."* Wash your lips gently and say: *"May I have confidence in my words so that other people can hear my true self and the beauty I hold within."*

7. As you slowly wash the rest of your face, say: *"May I have confidence in the way I look and feel about myself. Let my true beauty shine through for all to see and for me to feel. So mote it be."*

8. Finish washing your face. If you feel you need to, you can repeat a similar ritual with your moisturizer.

9. Take your normal amount of moisturizer, begin to rub it into your skin, and say these words: *"May this moisturizer enhance my beauty so that it radiates through so brightly, others can see it clearly. May it empower how I feel about myself and give me confidence in my beauty, both inside and out. So mote it be."*

Cosmetics Glamor Magick Spell

Best time to practice: Anytime

If you wear cosmetics, this is an easy spell to cast when you use your normal make-up. Each item of make-up can be magickally used for different things and it's up to you what you choose to wear.

TOOLS

Your usual make-up

METHOD

1. Cleanse your make up and space, then ground your energies.

2. Choose your make-up. Here are a few things to magickally use make-up for.

• Foundation/powder—as a protective mask. Self-protection is self-care and it allows you to charm these items as a way to protect yourself from any unwanted energies you might pick up through the day.

• Mascara/eyeliner/eyeshadow—for clarity of sight so you can see exactly what's going on around you, and how you can solve a problem.

• Lipstick/lip-gloss/lipliner—to charm you mouth so you can speak your truth, and eloquently put your feelings into words.

3. For foundation or powder: Visualize the white light of protection surrounding the make-up for a few moments, and say: *"I imbue this foundation/powder with protective power. I will apply it like a mask that protects me from negative energies, ill will, and any kind of unwanted energies."* Apply the make-up as you usually would, but as you do, visualize yourself painting on a protective mask. Visualize the product surrounded with white light as you apply, covering your face with this light.

4. For mascara, eyeliner, or eyeshadow: Hold the eye make-up and visualize yourself seeing things with absolute clarity. If there is a particular situation you want to have clarity of sight with, think of it for a few moments and say: *"I imbue this mascara/eyeliner/eyeshadow with the power of clarity. As I apply it to my eyes, may I see with clear sight and vision so I see things to be what they truly are."* Apply the make-up as you usually would, visualizing the make-up as white light that helps you to see any situation clearly.

5. For lipstick, lip-gloss, or lipliner: Hold the make-up for a few moments and visualize having the confidence and ability to speak your own truth. When you're ready, say: *"I imbue this lipstick/lip-gloss/lipliner with power to enable me to voice my truth. As I apply it, may it give me the confidence to speak up for myself and my needs."*

6. Once you've applied your make-up, look at yourself in the mirror and say *"So mote it be!"*

Mirror Ritual to See Your Authentic Self

Best time to practice: During a Waxing Moon, or on a Full Moon, New Moon, or Friday

Mirror magick can help you look into your own soul and see deeper, to embrace and give love to your authentic self. This ritual will help you see the person you are, and help connect with yourself.

INGREDIENTS
Rose quartz

TOOLS
Cleansing tools
Circle casting tools (optional)
Piece of paper and a pen
Mirror (any size, as long as it is big enough to see your face)

METHOD

1. Cleanse your tools and space.
2. Ground your energies, then cast a circle, if it is part of your practice.
3. Take the piece of paper and pen and write about the person you are. Write about both good and bad things—in order to connect with your authentic self, you need to see the whole picture, not just part of it.
4. Remember to write about the things you really are, not the things you want to be. Keep it grounded in reality.
5. When you're ready, sit in front of the mirror and look into your eyes. This may feel uncomfortable, but stick with it. Think of your reflection as another person if it makes it easier. If any negative thoughts come into your head as you look into the mirror, let them pass and don't hold on to them.
When you're ready, say these words: *"May this ritual show me who I truly am and introduce me to my authentic self. May it help me connect with the person I am to help me live my authentic life. I will love this person entirely because I am worthy and deserve to receive this love. So mote it be."*
6. Look in the mirror and give yourself a genuine smile, while thinking about giving loving energy to yourself. Look beyond the smile and your physical appearance to see your soul within.
7. Now take the paper and, keeping eye contact with yourself in the mirror, slowly read out all the things you have written down. By doing this, you are introducing yourself to who you truly are.
8. When you've finished reading, sit there for a few minutes, keeping eye contact with your reflection, and think about your authentic self who you've just been introduced to.
9. Hold the rose quartz in your hand and say: *"My authentic self is worthy of love, I deserve to give love to myself."*
10. Take some time to visualize this love flowing from the crystal and into your hands, then filling your entire body from the tips of your toes to the top of your head.
11. Open your circle.
12. Keep the crystal with you to help foster feelings of self-love toward your authentic self throughout your day.

CHAPTER 12

Psychic Abilities

Having psychic abilities is about being able to know the unknowable. We are all born with psychic gifts to different degrees but it's about how we identify, access, and strengthen these gifts that affects how we can hone these natural abilities within our own lives and Craft. This chapter contains a range of different spells and rituals to help make the most of your natural psychic abilities.

Divination Candle

Best time to practice: During a Waxing Moon, or on a Full Moon, New Moon, or Monday

Making your own candle is easier than you think! This candle is perfect to burn during divination sessions to help you tap into your intuitive powers and reach a higher state of consciousness.

INGREDIENTS
Purple food coloring (optional)
1 drop lavender essential oil
(to aid communication)
1 drop sandalwood essential oil
(to reach higher consciousness)
A sprinkle of mugwort
(to increase intuition)

TOOLS
Cleansing tools
1 purple or white tea light
(to enhance divinatory skills)
Bowl
A pan of hot water

METHOD

1. Cleanse your ingredients, tools, and space before you begin.
2. Ground your energy before you begin.
3. Take the tea light and remove it from the metal case, then carefully take out the wick from the bottom of the candle that is attached to a circular piece of metal. You'll need this later on.
4. Place the wax from the tea light into a bowl, then put the bowl on top of a pan of hot water on the stove on a medium heat until all the wax melts completely.
5. If using a white tea light, add the purple food coloring to the wax. Mix the wax until it has all turned purple.
6. Take the wick and put it back into the metal case of the tea light so the wick is pointing upward.
7. Gently pour the hot wax back into the metal case of the tea light.
8. Add the essential oils to the hot wax and then sprinkle a little mugwort on top.
9. Leave the wax to solidify before lighting during divination.

Develop the Clair Senses Spell

Best time to practice: During a Waxing Moon, or on a Full Moon or New Moon

This spell will help to develop all your clair senses and show you the senses that are already the strongest within you. It will also reveal which of these senses need more work to develop.

The 8 clair senses—clairvoyance (clear vision), clairempathy (clear emotions), clairsentience (clear feeling), clairtangency (clear sense of touch), claircognizance (clear knowing), clairaudience (clear hearing), clairsalience (clear smell), clairgustance (clear taste).

INGREDIENTS

1 tsp base oil such as grapeseed or sunflower oil

1 tsp dried rosemary (to increase psychic abilities)

8 fresh bay leaves (to enhance psychic abilities and manifestation)

TOOLS

Cleansing tools

Circle casting tools (optional)

Knife

1 purple candle (for developing psychic abilities)

Candleholder

Lighter or matches

Pen

Cauldron or heatproof dish

Notepad

METHOD

1. Cleanse your tools, herbs, and space.
2. Ground and center your energies, then cast a circle, if part of your practice.
3. Take some time to meditate on each of the clair senses. Focus on the intention of your spell: to develop these senses in your own Witchcraft practice, and to show you which of these senses are strongest for you.
4. Carve the words, "I develop my clair senses," into the candle wax.
5. Take a little oil and rub it on the candle in a clockwise direction.
6. Sprinkle rosemary over the candle so it sticks to the oil. You can also roll the oiled candle in the rosemary so it sticks. Place the candle in a holder and light it.
7. Take the 8 bay leaves and, on each one, write the name of each of the clair senses opposite on a separate bay leaf.
8. Take one of the bay leaves and burn it in the flame of the purple candle. Then put it in the cauldron or heatproof dish. Bay leaves spit when burned, so take care. Watch the size of the flame as the bay leaf burns. Is the flame large? Is it small? Does it crackle a lot? Does it dance a lot? Make some notes about how the bay leaf burns so you can compare it to the others at the end.
9. Burn the leaves in turn. Watch and make a few notes about how they burn.
10. Now you've burned them all, compare your notes. How did the burning leaves compare?
11. When you're comparing, listen to what your intuition is telling you, too.
12. Let the candle burn out, and open your circle.

> • Large flames suggest this clair sense is strong within you.
> • Small flames mean the clair sense needs developing since it's not as strong.
> • Dancing flames suggest this clair sense is already pretty developed.
> • Flames that go out quickly suggest the clair sense isn't your natural psychic ability.

Psychic Abilities Ointment

Best time to practice: During a Waxing Moon, or on a New Moon or Full Moon

This ointment, taken from my grimoire, will help to support any kind of psychic development and can be used to strengthen your natural psychic gifts. Use it to anoint yourself on your third eye (in between your eyebrows) and on your pulse points. It can be used before divination and before any spells or rituals connected to growing your psychic and spiritual abilities. Use it to anoint candles, crystals, and other ritual or spell items.

INGREDIENTS
2.5 oz (70 g) sunflower oil
4 tsp peppermint (to heighten psychic awareness)
4 tsp ground cinnamon (to stimulate psychic powers)
4 tsp thyme (to enhance natural psychic gifts)
Dried lemon peel (to sharpen psychic awareness and concentration)
0.5 oz (15 g) beeswax (for a vegan alternative, use 0.5 oz (15 g) candelilla wax)

TOOLS
Cleansing tools
Large jar with a lid
Pan of water
Glass bowl that fits over the pan
Container of your choice (such as a shallow jar or candle tin)

METHOD

1. Cleanse your tools, ingredients, and space.
2. Ground yourself before you begin.
3. Take your jar and add the oil, herbs, and spices. Leave this mixture for about 4–6 weeks so the dried ingredients can infuse the oil.
4. After this time, place water in a pan and bring it to a simmer. Put the beeswax or candelilla wax in a glass bowl, then put the bowl over the pan. Melt the wax down, being careful not to burn it. Keep stirring as it melts.
5. When it's completely melted, add the herb-infused oil, stirring to combine all the ingredients. You can leave the herbs in the salve or you can strain them out, depending on whether you want a rustic or cleaner look to the finished product. Do what feels right to you and your practice.
6. Once the oil and wax are mixed together, pour into your choice of container. Shallower containers tend to work better because it's easier to get to the salve. You can use shallow jars, clean lip balm tins, or candle tins—whatever you have to hand.
7. Leave your ointment to harden and then it is ready to use.

Talisman for Clearer Intuition

Best time to practice: During a Waxing Moon, or on a Full Moon or New Moon

Intuition is that deep inner knowing. Connecting the gap between the conscious and the subconscious mind, it helps you receive knowledge and understanding you could not possibly have known. This talisman will help to make the intuitive messages you receive clearer so you are able to understand them better. Wear the talisman (or, if it's a crystal, keep it with you) for at least a few weeks. During this time, listen to what your intuition and gut feelings are telling you.

INGREDIENTS

Lemongrass incense stick or cone (to sharpen intuition)
1 tsp dried rosemary (for clarity of sight)
Any piece of amethyst crystal or amethyst jewelry such as a pendant, ring, earrings, or necklace

TOOLS

Cleansing tools
Lighter or matches
Incense holder
Circle casting tools (optional)
3 purple candles (for psychic abilities)
Lighter or matches

METHOD

1. Cleanse your tools and workspace. Light your incense and place in a holder. Start by grounding and centering your energy, then cast a circle, if it is part of your practice.

2. Place the 3 candles in a triangle shape and place your piece of jewelry in the middle. Light the candles.

3. Sit for a time, focusing on the intention of the spell. Visualize your intuition giving you clearer intuitive messages as you wear or carry the talisman you're about to create, so you are able to fully understand them. Visualize this clarity increasing as you wear or carry your talisman.

4. When you're ready, sprinkle the rosemary over your piece of jewelry or crystal, and say: *"I enchant this piece of jewelry/crystal to bring me clearer intuition. Open up my third eye so that I may fully understand the messages my intuition brings. So mote it be."*

5. Sit there as the candles burn out, focusing on your talisman and the intention it was made with.

6. Put on the piece of jewelry or put the crystal in your pocket.

7. Let the candle burn out, and open your circle.

Crystal Grid to Strengthen Psychic Abilities

Best time to practice: During a Waxing Moon or a Full Moon

This crystal grid will help to strengthen and enhance you natural psychic abilities. This is a great grid to make when you are working to develop your psychic gifts, since it will gently strengthen your abilities over time. The pattern opposite is called the Flower of Life. It represents the interconnectedness of all beings, the framework of our entire universe, and the cycles of life. Placing your crystals on this grid will help channel the energies to magnify your intentions. Just a note, a crystal grid needs at least four crystals to be effective, so the more you use, the better! Check page 179 for other crystals you might have that would be good to use, too.

INGREDIENTS

Amethyst (to strengthen natural psychic gifts)
Labradorite (to expand awareness)
Lapis lazuli (to manifest psychic abilities)
Clear quartz (to amplify the energies of the other crystals)

TOOLS

Piece of paper and a pen
A photo or image of the Flower of Life

METHOD

1. Cleanse your tools, crystals, and space.
2. Ground your energies before you start.
3. Take a small piece of paper and write the words, "Strengthen my natural psychic abilities." Lay it on a flat surface where your grid won't be disturbed.
4. Place your copy of the Flower of Life on top of the piece of paper.
5. In the middle of the Flower of Life, place a piece of amethyst.
6. Arrange the other crystals in a pattern on the grid in a design that speaks to you, based on the number of crystals you use.
7. When you create your crystal grid, you might like to say a mantra along the lines of, "*My psychic abilities are growing and strengthened,*" so you can keep your intentions focused.
8. Once you're happy where all the crystals are placed, say these words: "*May this crystal grid help to strengthen and enhance my natural psychic abilities. So mote it be.*"
9. To activate your grid, use your index finger to draw an invisible line between one crystal to the next, to connect them all so the energy can flow between them.
10. Leave your grid where it is, undisturbed, until you feel your psychic abilities have strengthened.

Flying Oil

Best time to practice: On a Full Moon

Flying oils have been used by Witches for centuries to help induce a trance-like state that would aid their spiritual practices. Traditional recipes for flying oils would contain hallucinogenic/poisonous plants, which were applied to the skin in order to experience a "flying" experience. Thankfully, modern flying oils are completely safe, and don't contain any baneful products. They can still be used to help to create an altered state of awareness that can enhance and assist with meditation, lucid dreaming, astral projection, and visualization to name but a few.

INGREDIENTS

3 tsp dried mugwort, ground (to enhance intuition and psychic abilities)
3 tsp dried yarrow, ground (increasing psychic abilities)
3 tsp poppy seeds, ground (help to create altered state)
3 dried bay leaves, ground (psychic work)
12 fl oz (350 ml) base oil such as grapeseed or sunflower oil

TOOLS
Cleansing tools
Dropper bottle

METHOD

1. Cleanse your tools, ingredients, and space.
2. Ground your energies before you start.
3. Place the herbs into the jar, making sure to crumble up the bay leaves.
4. Fill up the rest of the jar with your chosen oil.
5. Secure the lid and give the jar a shake to mix up the oil and herbs.
6. Leave in a cool, dark place for 4 weeks. Remember to shake the bottle daily to help the herbs infuse the oil.
7. After 4 weeks, strain all the herbs from the oil and discard them.
8. Now your oil is ready to use. Use it to anoint your third eye (between your eyebrows), to assist with astral projection, or to practice trance work.

Divination Tea

This tea has been created to drink before (and during) any kind of divinatory practice in order to increase your sense of intuition and boost your natural psychic abilities. The tea will also help you to understand the messages that come through more clearly within your own divinatory practices.

INGREDIENTS
Kettle of hot water
2 tsp dried lemon balm (to increase intuition)
2 tsp dried thyme (to help develop your natural psychic power)
2 tsp dried dandelion (for divination)
2 tsp ground cinnamon (for understanding)
1 dried bay leaf (for clarity of sight)

TOOLS
Cleansing tools
Tea ball strainer
Mug
Jar with a lid or airtight container

METHOD

1. Cleanse your ingredients, tools, and workspace.
2. Ground your energy.
3. Combine all the ingredient in an airtight container and mix them well.
4. Put a teaspoon of all the ingredients into a tea ball strainer and close it up.
5. Heat up water until it's hot but not boiling and fill up your mug.
6. Put the strainer in your mug and leave to steep for 5–7 minutes.
7. Before you drink it, say, *"As I drink this tea, may these herbs and spices increase my divinatory sight, give a boost to my own psychic abilities, and help me see with clarity the messages that come to me at this time. So mote it be."*
8. Drink your tea!

Note: All herbal teas must be taken with caution by anyone taking prescribed medication. Check with your medical herbalist or doctor before drinking this tea, and avoid if pregnant.

CHAPTER 13

Ancestors, Spirits & Goddesses

In this chapter, you'll find spells and rituals that help you connect to and communicate with your ancestors, to build a relationship and communicate with a variety of different spirits, and to work with some very powerful goddess such as Hecate and Lilith. Working with ancestors, spirits, or any deity can be a part of your Witchcraft practice, but if working with them doesn't feel right or call to you, it's not something that you have to do within your own Craft. Do what feels right to you!

Freyja Spell for Inner Strength

Best time to practice: On Friday the 13th (Freyja's day) or a Full Moon

The Norse goddess Freyja is associated with beauty, fertility, sex, love, death, Witchcraft, and war. This powerful flower essence makes use of flowers that bring inner strength. It also makes use of selected runes as a way to add power and include Freyja's energies in the spell.

INGREDIENTS

The petals from 1 sunflower
(for strength and determination)
The petals from 3 chrysanthemum
flowers (for endurance
and perseverance)
The petals from 3 calendula flowers
(for resilience)
The following runes copied onto a
piece of paper: Uruz (for strength),
Fehu (Freyja's rune), Naudhiz (for
coming through struggles), Elhaz
(for protection and connect to
higher self)

TOOLS

Cleansing tools
Circle casting tools (optional)
Medium-sized bowl, half filled
with water
Sieve
Jar with a lid
Spray bottle

METHOD

1. Cleanse your tools, flowers, and workspace.
2. Start by grounding and centering your energies, then cast a circle, if it is part of your practice.
3. Take the heads from the flowers and place them in the bowl of water.
4. Lay the paper with the runes out in front of you and say: *"Freyja, you've shown so much strength in your life, I call upon you to fill me with inner strength so I can handle this strife. Freyja come to me, fill me with perseverance and resilience, let me learn from your experience. Fill me with endurance and determination, to make me strong in this situation. So mote it be."*
5. Place the paper in the water with the flowers. As the flowers go soft, they add their magickal energies to the essence.
6. Leave the bowl in the Sun for at least 4–5 hours, in order for the flowers and runes to infuse the water.
7. After this time, drain away the flowers and paper by passing the water through the sieve and collecting it into a jar or bottle.
8. Store in a cool dark place.
9. Open your circle.
10. Spray your body and your space whenever you need a boost of strength.

Spirits of the Land Ritual

Best time to practice: Anytime

This ritual will help you to connect to the local spirits of the land where you live in a respectful way. If you live in an area different to your ancestral home you can still honor the land and the spirits where you live now.

INGREDIENTS

An offering of your choice (based on your own culture or the culture of the place you live) for the spirits. This could include: water, alcohol, coffee, herbs, flowers, or food native to the land. Just make sure your offering is environmentally friendly and won't harm local wildlife.

TOOLS

Cleansing tools
1 white tea light (for spirituality)
Lighter or matches
Cauldron or heatproof dish

METHOD

1. This ritual can be performed in your yard, somewhere local like a forest, or anywhere outside you feel a particular call toward.
2. Go outside and find somewhere comfortable to sit. Take your time to ground your energy before opening yourself up to the energies and presences there. Look around at the natural world around you, listen to all the different sounds you can hear, and all the aromas you can smell. Immerse yourself fully in the place where you are.
3. When you're ready, light the tea light, placing it safely in your cauldron or heatproof dish. Make sure your cauldron or disc is stable on the ground so it won't fall over. Don't leave the candle unattended.
4. Take your time to introduce yourself to the spirits.
5. After you've finished speaking, sit and listen to any responses that might come from the natural world around you (like a gust of wind when you ask a question), any thoughts that pop up into your mind, or intuitive messages you receive.
6. When you're ready, give your offerings by placing what you've brought in a place you feel is suitable, whether that be a tree stump, the base of a tree, or somewhere else that calls to you. If you have brought a liquid offering, pour it into the ground if appropriate.
7. If you're not sure what offerings to leave for the spirits of the land where you are, ask them to show you! Take time to listen and speak to them and watch for signs of the offerings they want.
8. When you're ready to leave, thank the spirits for their time and energy and say goodbye. Extinguish the tea light if it's still alight.
9. Keep visiting the same place and spending time there. Take an offering each time. The more time you spend there, the more your relationship with the spirits of the land will grow.

Hecate Ritual for Boundary Setting

Best time to practice: On a Full Moon or Wednesday

This ritual calls upon Hecate, the goddess of magick and the underworld. Hecate is associated with keys since it is said she holds the keys that can unlock the gates between realms. This makes her a great goddess to work with if you want to set boundaries. This spell will help you to set necessary boundaries for the sake of your own well-being, which is particularly helpful if you find boundary setting difficult.

INGREDIENTS
½ tsp dried poppy seeds, ground (for setting inner boundaries)
½ tsp dried yarrow, ground (to maintain integrity when boundary setting)
½ tsp dried nettle, ground (for setting boundaries with others)
1 tsp dried dandelion leaves and flowers, ground (as an offering for Hecate)

TOOLS
Cleansing tools
Circle casting tools (optional)
Charcoal disc
Lighter or matches
Cauldron or heatproof dish
A key or image of a key

METHOD

1. Cleanse all tools and your workspace.
2. Start by grounding and centering your energy, then casting a circle, if it is part of your practice.
3. Place the charcoal disc into the cauldron or heatproof dish. Light the charcoal disc until it begins to spark and leave it until it begins to turn white.
4. Mix the herbs well, then add to the cauldron, placing them on top of the charcoal disc so it releases smoke.
5. Take the key, pass it through the smoke of the incense and then hold it in your hands. Focus on the areas of your life where you want to set boundaries. Think about how you want help setting these boundaries.
6. When you're ready, say this incantation: *"Hecate, Hecate, keeper of the keys, I ask you to help me set healthy boundaries. Where I struggle, give me courage in my actions. Let me set boundaries for the sake of my well-being and satisfaction. With this key, it will remain for me a symbol of the boundaries I must set, So that in my life, I can get my needs met. So mote it be."*
7. Keep the key with you when you need to set boundaries with others or if you are around those who ignore the boundaries you have already set.
8. Open your circle.
9. Let the charcoal cool completely before cleaning away the ashes and leftover herbs.

Connecting to Your Ancestors Ritual

Best time to practice: Anytime you want to connect with your ancestors

This ritual will help you to communicate with your loved ones who have passed, both the ancestors you have known in their physical form and also ancestors who have gone way before you.

INGREDIENTS

1 tsp dried mugwort, ground (to enhance psychic abilities to aid communication)
1 tsp dried pine needles, ground (to connect to your ancestors)
1 tsp dried rosemary, ground (for remembrance of the dead)
1 tsp base oil, such as grapeseed or sunflower oil
An offering of water or your ancestors' favorite food or drink

TOOLS

Cleansing tools
Circle casting tools (optional)
Mortar and pestle
1 black candle (for spirit work)
Lighter or matches
Something that comes from the ancestor(s) you wish to communicate with
Piece of paper and a pen

METHOD

1. Gather all your ingredients together and cleanse them thoroughly.
2. Ground your energies and cast a circle, if it is part of your practice.
3. In a mortar and pestle, grind the herbs down into a powder and sprinkle them on a flat surface.
4. Cover the candle in a little oil, then roll it in the herbs.
5. Light the candle.
6. As it burns, take a piece of paper and take your time to write a letter to your ancestors. Talk to them as if they were still alive and with you now. Tell them how you're doing but don't forget to ask them how they're doing. Talk about any recent achievements, how things are going in life, and any problems you're having, asking them for any advice or opinions.
7. When you've finished, fold up the paper and seal it with a kiss, then burn it over the candle flame to release your words so your ancestors may hear you.
8. As it burns, say this incantation: *"As I speak these words, hear the message I send. May they reach you quickly and with love, with these words I've penned. So mote it be."*
9. Open your circle.
10. Keep vigilant for any ways your ancestors might try to reply to your letter. Looks for signs and make sure you listen to your intuition.

Spirit Communication Incense

Best time to practice: On a New Moon, Full Moon, Wednesday, or Samhain

Burning this incense will help to create the perfect atmosphere to help you connect with those in spirit since it opens channels for clearer communication between this world and the next. This incense also offers protection to help ward off any evil spirits coming forward, keeping you safe from any negativity. Use this during any kind of spirit work.

INGREDIENTS

1 tsp dried mugwort, ground (for spirit communication)
1 tsp dried yarrow, ground (to ward off any negative spirits)
1 tsp dried vervain, ground (to aid spirit work and communication
1 tsp dried wormwood, ground (for protection and calling spirits)

TOOLS

Cleansing tools
Cauldron or heatproof dish
Charcoal disc
Lighter or matches
Jar

METHOD

1. Cleanse your herbs, tools, and space.
2. Ground your energy.
3. Take time to magickally cleanse your home well in all rooms.
4. Place all the herbs into the jar and mix them up thoroughly.
5. Place the charcoal disc into the cauldron or heatproof dish. Light the charcoal disc until it begins to spark and leave it until it begins to turn white.
6. Say these words as you add a teaspoon of your loose herb incense onto the disc to release the smoke and aromas into your home: *"I seek to respectfully communicate with the spirits in this house. I seek to honor and build a relationship with them. May this incense open channels between this world and the world beyond to make this communication possible. May it help me understand the messages the spirits bring. I am protected from those negative or evil spirits who wish to do me harm, they may not approach me. So mote it be."*
7. Burn the incense on its own or as part of a spell or ritual in order to help you contact spirits.
8. Let the incense burn out and fully cool before disposing of it. Store the incense that remains in a jar for later use.

Household Spirit Communication Ritual

Best time to practice: On a Full Moon, New Moon, Wednesday, or Samhain

Every household has spirits that are the soul of the house. To keep a happy home, it's important to build up a relationship with these spirits through communication. Using automatic writing is a good practice to enable you to communicate with the spirits of your home.

INGREDIENTS

Spirit communication incense
(page 140)
Black tourmaline
Black obsidian (for protection
during automatic writing)

TOOLS

Cleansing tools
Circle casting tools (optional)
Charcoal disc
Cauldron or heatproof dish
Lighter or matches
1 black candle (for protection)
Piece of paper and a pen

METHOD

1. Cleanse your tools, ingredients, and space.
2. Take some time to ground yourself and cast a circle—this is vital for spirit work to help protect you from negative spirits.
3. Place the charcoal disc into the cauldron or heatproof dish. Light the charcoal disc until it begins to spark. Leave it until it begins to turn white. Burn the loose spirit communication incense on top.
4. Light the black candle and place the crystals near to where you'll be doing your automatic writing as protection.
5. Sit somewhere comfortable and introduce yourself to the spirits of the house. Ask the spirits to use their energy to communicate with you if they wish. You must always be respectful—don't command them.
6. Visualize yourself surrounded by bright white light and say these words: *"May the spirits of this house speak to me through my pen. May they communicate with me in a way I can understand. Any negative, evil or malicious spirits are not welcome here in my house, and I forbid them to channel their energy through me. I am protected, these spirits may not approach me. I open the doors to all benevolent spirits only. So mote it be."*
7. Write the questions you would like an answer to on the paper, leaving adequate room for the answers when you start the automatic writing.
8. Starting at the first question, hold your pen lightly in your hand over the blank space and ask the question out loud to get the energy flowing. Close your eyes and start drawing spirals. Move the pen in the direction that feels right and go with the flow of energy.
9. Open your eyes to see what is written on the paper. The messages you receive may be difficult to decipher, but they will get clearer the more you commune with your household spirits.
10. At the end of the session, thank the spirits for their energy and effort.
11. Open your circle.

Hecate Candle Spell for Ancestor Communication

Best time to practice: On Samhain night, or during October

Hecate is the Greek goddess of Witchcraft, magick, and the underworld and is often known as the Queen of Witches. She is also referred to as the Queen of the Night and can help you contact the spirits of your departed loved ones. This candle spell calls upon this aspect of Hecate's powers in order to put you in touch with your ancestors. This spell is best cast when the veil between the living and the dead is at its thinnest on Samhain night but also when the veil is thinning during October.

INGREDIENTS

1 tsp salt
1 fl oz (30 ml) water
1 tsp fresh or dried rosemary, chopped
An offering such as wine, water, honey, bread, lavender, or poppy seeds, for Hecate

TOOLS

Cleansing tools
Circle casting tools (optional)
Spray bottle
1 black candle (for protection)
Lighter or matches
Notebook and pen

METHOD

1. Cleanse the things you need to cast the spell.
2. Ground and center your own energies then cast a circle, if it is part of your practice.
3. In a spray bottle, dissolve the salt in water to make a saltwater solution.
4. Put the rosemary into the spray bottle with the saltwater.
5. Take the candle and hold the wick before lightly spraying the candle for protection against any negative spirits that may draw near.
6. If you don't have pets, you can also use the saltwater to lightly spray the area you are doing the spell in.
7. Light the candle and say this incantation: "*Hekate, Hekate, Queen of the Night, bring forth the spirits of my loved ones tonight. As this candle's flame burns bright, bring the spirits of my ancestors into my sight. So mote it be.*"
8. Gaze at the flame and say the names of the loved ones who have passed, who you want to communicate with, out loud.
9. Continue to gaze at the flame and keep your mind open to any words, phrases, feelings, and names that pop into your mind at this time.
10. When you're ready to finish, thank the spirits and Hecate for their help and energy.
11. Blow the candle out and write down any messages you received.
12. Leave out an offering such as wine, water, honey, bread, lavender, or poppy seeds, to thank Hecate.
13. Open your circle.

Lilith Empowerment Spell

Best time to practice: On a Dark Moon, New Moon, Full Moon, or at night

According to folklore, God made Lilith (not Eve) as the first woman to be a companion for Adam. However, Lilith would not submit to Adam, feeling they were created equal. As a consequence, she was banished from the Garden of Eden and is known as a symbol of liberation and empowerment. This spell will call on Lilith's power to fill you with empowered energies. If you feel you've given away too much of your own power recently and want to call it back to you, this spell will help you to do this too.

INGREDIENTS

Dragon's blood incense or resin (to honor Lilith and boost the potency of your magick)
1 tsp dried vervain (for empowerment)
1 tsp dried mugwort (to connect with Lilith's powers of empowerment and liberty)
1 tsp ground cinnamon (to invoke Lilith's powers)
A handful of dried red or pink rose petals (as an offering to Lilith)
An offering such as apples, cinnamon sticks, a small mirror, water, or wine, for Lilith

TOOLS

Lighter or matches
Incense holder
Cleansing tools
Circle casting tools (optional)
Mortar and pestle
Piece of paper
1 red candle (for association with Lilith)
Candleholder

METHOD

1. Light the dragon's blood incense in an incense holder and cleanse your tools and ingredients.
2. Ground your energy and cast a circle, if it is part of your practice.
3. Using a mortar and pestle, grind down the vervain, mugwort, and cinnamon. Place the piece of paper on a flat surface, and sprinkle the herbs onto it. Smooth them out into a thin layer.
4. Hold the candle by the wick, and gently melt the wax around the candle so it softens enough for the herbs to stick to it. When the wax has softened, roll the candle in the herbs sprinkled on the paper until the candle is covered in the herbal mixture.
5. Place the candle in a holder. Sprinkle the rose petals around the candle as a gift to Lilith before you ask for her assistance.
6. Light the candle and sit for a moment, focusing on the flame.
7. When you're ready, say these words three times: *"Lilith I come to you, the goddess of the night, empower me in all areas of my life. Bring me confidence and strength to empower my mind, body, and spirit, and where I have given my power away to others, I call it back this minute. So mote it be."*
8. Watch the candle burn as you focus on the flame. Feel Lilith's empowering energy through your whole body.
9. When you have finished, thank Lilith for her presence and energy. Leave a small offering near the candle as gratitude for her assistance.
10. Let the candle burn out, then open your circle.

CHAPTER 14

Hearth, Home & Kitchen Witchery

Our homes are our sanctuaries. Creating the right atmosphere and welcoming in the right kind of energies into our home is important because we want them to be places of safety in both a physical and spiritual sense. Kitchen witchery is often an integral part of Witchcraft in the home environment for many Witches. Through spells, rituals, folk charms, and recipes, this chapter will help you care for your home on an energetic level so you can create the kind of atmosphere you want to live in.

Herbal Happy Home Jar

The herbs used in this spell jar will help to raise the vibrations in your home to attract happiness and all good energy, helping to create a light and harmonious home environment.

INGREDIENTS
1 tsp dried lavender (for comfort and calm)
1 tsp dried rose petals (for tranquillity)
1 tsp dried lemon balm (to boost the mood of your home)
1 tsp dried basil (to release any negativity in your home)
1 tsp dried peppermint (to raise energetic vibrations in your home)

TOOLS
Cleansing tools
Circle casting tools (optional)
Jar with lid
1 yellow candle (for happiness)
Lighter or matches

METHOD
1. Cleanse your herbs, tools, and space.
2. Ground yourself and cast a circle, if it is part of your practice.
3. Take your jar and fill it with the ingredients. As you do, focus on your intentions of creating a happy home.
4. When you've finished, secure the lid so it's tightly closed.
5. Hold the bottle in your hands, and say: *"Bring happiness to my home, raise the vibrations in this place, any negativity and unwanted energies are swiftly replaced. So mote it be."*
6. Light the yellow candle and drip hot wax around the lid of the jar to seal it.
7. Keep the jar in the room you spend the most time in and let its energies gently and gradually fill your home.

Sweep Away Negative Energies Broom Spell

Best time to practice:
Whenever you want to remove
negative energies from your home

Using a broom or besom is an ancient way of removing any negative and unwanted energies from your home. The sweeping action in this spell will also help to release any stagnant energies that have been hanging around, to bring feelings of peace and lightness to your home and those who inhabit it.

TOOLS
Home cleaning tools
Cleansing tools
Broom

METHOD
1. Ground yourself before you begin.
2. Take some time to go around your house, cleaning and tidying up.
3. Magickally cleanse your broom, opening your back door or a window so the negative energies have a place they can exit your home from.
4. Since this is an energetic clean, there is no need to actually sweep the floor. When you sweep, hover the broom a little above the floor. Starting in the room furthest away from the open door or window, sweep in one corner, and then work in a counter-clockwise direction around the outside of the room, from one corner to another. Still working in a counter-clockwise direction, sweep around the room from the outside toward the center.
5. Repeat this practice in each room of your home, working your way closer to the open back door or window.
6. When you get to the door, sweep out all the negative energy you've collected. As you do, say: *"All negativity is swept away, all stagnant energy is released. There is nothing but good energies here, feelings of peace and happiness increased. So mote it be."*

Cinnamon Home Prosperity Spell

Best time to practice:
At the start of every week or month

This simple prosperity spell will help to draw money toward you and your home.

INGREDIENTS
1 tsp ground cinnamon (to draw wealth and prosperity)

TOOLS
Cleansing tools

METHOD
1. Ground your energies before you begin.
2. Place the ground cinnamon in your hand and go and stand just behind the threshold of your open front door.
3. Magickally cleanse the doorway and the cinnamon.
4. When you're ready, say these words: *"When this cinnamon smoke blows, prosperity flows. It enters my life and this house, may it never go. So mote it be."*
5. Blow the cinnamon over the threshold and out of your front door.

Home Protection Hag Stone Charm

Best time to practice:
On a Full Moon or Saturday

It's important to protect the place you live in from negative and unwanted energies. Using a hag stone, this charm will help to bring protection as well as good luck and healing to your home. Hag stones have naturally occurring holes through them and have been used for centuries in folk protection magick.

TOOLS
Cleansing tools
1 hag stone
A length of red string or garden twine

METHOD
1. Cleanse your tools.
2. Ground your energies before you begin.
3. Take the string and place it through the hole in the hag stone. Tie a knot in the string so the stone is secure. As you tie the knot, say: *"May this hag stone bring protection upon this home, both physically and energetically. Let nothing come through this door that is harmful and negative in any way. So mote it be."*
4. Make a loop with the rest of the string so the hag stone can be hung up.
5 . Hang it up near your front door, either inside or outside.

Finding a New Home Spell

Best time to practice: On a New Moon or Full Moon

Finding the perfect house or apartment for you (and the people you live with) in the right place isn't easy. If you're searching for a new place to live, this spell jar can help you find the kind of home you're searching for and speed up the process of finding it.

INGREDIENTS

1 dried bay leaf (for manifestation)
1 tsp ground cinnamon (for success)
1 tsp ground coffee (to speed up house hunting and for power)
1 tsp dried basil, ground (for money and a harmonious home)
1 tsp dried oregano, ground (for a happy home)
1 tsp dried lavender, ground (for a calm and peaceful home)
Enough sugar to fill half your fabric pouch (to sweeten the deal)

TOOLS

Cleansing tools
Circle casting tools (optional)
Piece of paper and a pen
Brown fabric pouch with a tie
House key (an old, unused key is fine)

METHOD

1. Cleanse your tools, ingredients, and space.
2. Ground yourself and cast a circle, if it is part of your practice.
3. Take a few moments to visualize the kind of home you want or need, how it will change your life by moving there, and how you will feel.
4. When you're ready, place all the ingredients except the sugar in the pouch.
5. Write a list of everything you want from your new house, within your price range: size, location, number of bedrooms and bathrooms, outside space, and anything else you are specifically looking for. Go into as much detail as you can about your wants and needs. When you've finished, fold it up and put it into your pouch.
6. Whatever sized pouch you're using, fill it with enough sugar so it's half full.
7. Hold the pouch underneath, so it has some stability, and push the key down into the sugar, like putting it in the lock of your new home. Turn the key in the sugar as if you are opening the front door, and say:
  "May this key unlock the door to the home I/we desire, May it bring to me/us the home I/we require. So mote it be."
8. Tie the pouch tight and secure so it won't come loose.
9. Open your circle.
10. Keep the pouch with you when you are house hunting or doing anything related to finding your new home.

Simmer Pot to Remove Bad Atmosphere

Best time to practice: Whenever you need to remove a bad atmosphere in your home

Whether it's an unwanted or toxic visitor or an argument within the home, the negative energies they create can leave a bad atmosphere. This simmer pot will help to restore a sense of peace and calm within your home.

INGREDIENTS

Water

3 cinnamon sticks (to purify and raise the vibration of your spell)

6 cloves (to drive away negativity and attract positive energies into your home)

2 tbs dried lavender (to bring peace and calm)

1 orange (to bring happiness into your home)

3 dried bay leaves (for protection)

TOOLS

Cleansing tools

Saucepan

Spoon

Spray bottle

METHOD

1. Cleanse your ingredients, tools, and workspace.
2. Start by grounding and centering your energies.
3. Add your ingredients into your saucepan and say out loud what each of the ingredients will bring to your spell, such as, *"I use this cinnamon to purify my home."*
4. Fill the saucepan with water so it covers all the ingredients.
5. Using a spoon, stir the water in a counter-clockwise direction for a few moments to symbolize removal of the bad atmosphere. As you do, say: *"With the aromas of this simmer pot, I remove the bad atmosphere in this house. This energy is not welcome here. So mote it be."*
6. Then stir the water in a clockwise direction to symbolize drawing positive energy, peace, and happiness into your home in their place, and say: *"Now the bad atmosphere is gone, I welcome in peace, happiness, calm, and all positive energies in its place. So mote it be."*
7. Put the pot on a low heat and leave to simmer for at least 3 hours, or as long as you need to until you feel that the bad atmosphere has been removed. Add more water to the pot as necessary so it doesn't boil dry. Let the aromas permeate your home to restore the energy there.
8. When finished, let the water cool. You can drain away the ingredients and put the water in a spray bottle, where you can use it if you need extra help to remove any bad atmosphere from your home. Use within 1 week.

Magickal Herbs Ritual

Best time to practice: During a Waxing Moon, or on a New Moon, Full Moon, or Thursday

Growing herbs inside your home, like on a bright windowsill, can help to attract different kinds of energies to your home, depending on the herbs you choose to grow. These herbs can also be used to add intention to your cooking and for spell and ritual work. This spell uses three of my favorite herbs to grow inside but you can grow whatever plants attract the kind of energies you want to fill your home with. Just check they will thrive indoors first and how much water they'll need. When they get too big for their pot, plant them in a bigger pot or plant outside. You can grow them from seed or buy already established plants from stores and nurseries.

INGREDIENTS
1 potted basil plant (for luck and abundance)
1 potted thyme plant (to repel negative energies)
1 potted oregano plant (to bring happiness, love, and protection)
3 clear quartz (to amplify the energies of other crystals and keep the plant healthy)
3 moss agate (to help the plants grow)
3 tiger's eye (to support growth)

TOOLS
Cleansing tools

METHOD

1. Cleanse your plants, crystals, and space.
2. Ground your energy.
3. Take the plants and stand them in a line in front of you.
4. Hold the basil plant in your hand and say: *"May this basil plant bring luck and abundance into my home and into the lives of those who live here. So mote it be."*
5. Hold the thyme plant in your hand, and say: *"May this thyme plant repel any negative energies away from my home and bring courage and strength to all beings that reside here. So mote it be."*
6. Hold the oregano plant and say: *"May this oregano plant attract feelings of happiness and love into my home as well as bring protection to this place and all who live here. So mote it be."*
7. Take the crystals and push a piece of clear quartz, moss agate, and tiger's eye around the plant, into the soil of each pot. When you've done this, say: *"May these crystals promote good health and encourage strong growth. So mote it be."*
8. Place the herbs in a warm place that gets plenty of sun, such as a kitchen windowsill.

Magickal Kitchen Cleanser

Best time to practice: On a New Moon, Full Moon, or Monday

Due to its antibacterial and antimicrobial properties, this kitchen cleanser can be used to wash kitchen floors, or kitchen surfaces. It also brings protection and a boost in mood to those in your home.

INGREDIENTS
25 fl oz (750 ml) water
6 sprigs of fresh rosemary or 3 tsp dried rosemary (for protection and energetic cleansing)
6 drops of orange, lemon, or grapefruit essential oil, or the peel of 1 orange (to lift the mood of the house)

TOOLS
Cleansing tools
Saucepan
Sieve (if using dried rosemary)
Spray bottle

METHOD

1. Cleanse your ingredients, tools, and space.
2. Ground your energies before you start.
3. Add the water to the pan and, on a low heat, bring it to a simmer.
4. Add the rosemary and essential oil or orange peel and stir it clockwise three times for attraction.
5. Let it simmer for about 30 minutes before taking it off the heat and allow to cool completely.
6. Once cooled, take out the orange peel and sprigs of rosemary. If you have used dried rosemary, use a sieve to drain it from the water.
7. Pour it into a spray bottle and use in your kitchen. You can also use the water with a mop to wash the floors in your home. Use within 3 weeks.

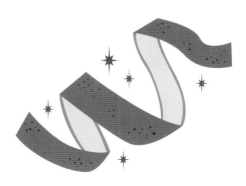

Buying Your Own Home Spell

Best time to practice: The night before you put in an offer

If you want a specific house or apartment that's for sale, this spell will help to give you a magickal boost when trying to buy it. This spell will only work when you are realistic about the house you have your eye on. It won't manifest you a house worth millions unless this is realistic for you.

INGREDIENTS
1 tsp dried rosemary, ground (to attract the money you need to buy the home)
1 tsp dried basil, ground (for luck and success)
1 tsp ground nutmeg (for prosperity and abundance)
1 tsp ground cinnamon (for good fortune and new opportunities)
Small amount of dirt from the outside space of the house you want to buy

TOOLS
Cleansing tools
Circle casting tools (optional)
A photo of the house printed on paper
Pen

METHOD

1. Cleanse your ingredients, tools, and space.
2. Start by grounding and centering your energies, then casting a circle, if it is part of your practice.
3. Take a few moments to focus on your intention, to buy your house.
4. On a flat surface, lay out the paper with the house you want.
5. Write your name on the house in the photo, and the name of anyone else you may be buying the house with.
6. Write, "I own this house, it is already mine" three times horizontally on the house. Turn the paper 90 degrees and vertically write, "My offer will be accepted."
7. Look at the price it's on the market for and make a reasonable and sensible offer you are willing to pay. Write the monetary figure you are offering for it. Then say: *"This house I seek is mine already, I've made a fair offer and to move in I'm ready. I attract it toward me with all of my might, My offer will be accepted as I weave this spell tonight."*
8. Mix the dirt with the herbs and then sprinkle them over the house on the paper and say: *"I/we own this house, of this I/we have no doubts, on this day, this I/we announce! So mote it be."*
9. Leave the photo, herbs, and dirt on the flat surface as you keep manifesting the house you want.
10. Open your circle.

Home Boundaries Protection Spell

Best time to practice: On a New Moon or Full Moon

Your home is a place of sanctuary and it's very important that you protect it magickally from any negative unwanted energies, ill intent, or trespassers. This folk spell will help to protect your space.

INGREDIENTS

3 tsp dried rosemary, ground (to banish negative energies)
3 tsp dried nettle, ground (for boundary defence)
3 tsp dried comfrey, ground (for home protection)
4 peeled cloves of garlic (to neutralize bad energy)
Protection oil (see page 91)

TOOLS

Cleansing tools
Circle casting tools (optional)
Container
4 iron nails (for protection)
Hammer

METHOD

1. Cleanse your tools, ingredients, and space.
2. Ground yourself and your energies, then cast a circle, if it is part of your practice.
3. Add all the ingredients except the oil into a container and stir them to mix them up. Place the garlic cloves on top.
4. Take the iron nails one at a time and anoint them with the protection oil. Visualize each one's protective power as you rub it in oil, and say: *"With this nail of iron, my home is protected, toward my home this power is directed. It marks the boundaries of my home, It protects it in every direction again the unknown. So mote it be."*
5. Repeat this process with all four nails.
6. When you're ready, take the herbs, nails, and the hammer and go outside into your yard. If you don't have an outdoor space, complete this process by placing them in all four corners of your home.
7. If casting this spell inside your home, go to the four corners of the room and place a nail on the floor in each corner. If casting this spell outside, hammer a nail into the ground in each corner of your garden or property
8. Sprinkle a quarter of the herbs around the nail, placing a clove of garlic on top.
9. Move around your yard or living space in a clockwise direction to attract protection, knocking all four nails into all four corners, sprinkling the herbs, and placing a clove of garlic as per step 8.
10. Visualize the white light of protection coming from all four nails and covering your home in a dome of energy for a few minutes. As the white light gets brighter, so does the protection. When you're ready, say out loud: *"My spell is cast. So mote it be."*
11. Open your circle.

CHAPTER 15

Family & Friends

Friends and family are the people we share our time and energy with. These personal relationships form the central part of our lives in one form or another and we can use magick to strengthen these relationships, mend them when they're broken, and help them when they are in need. This chapter contains spells and rituals to enable you to connect with your friends and family on a deeper level.

Family & Friends Fire Protection

Best time to practice: During a Waxing Moon, or on a Full Moon or Saturday

The desire to protect those we love is natural and, as Witches, we can use magick to surround our friends and family with protection. This spell can be cast for one or more of your loved ones to bring physical, emotional, and energetic protection. It uses herbs aligned with the element Fire in order to surround them with the fiery light of protection.

INGREDIENTS

Dragon's blood incense cone or stick (to protect by driving away negativity)
1 tsp chili flakes (for energetic protection)
1 tsp ground black pepper (for physical protection)
1 clove per person (for spiritual protection)
1 chrysanthemum flower (for mental protection)
Pyrite
Tiger's eye

TOOLS

Lighter and matches
Incense holder
Cleansing tools
Circle casting tools (optional)
Photographs of the family members you want to protect
1 black candle (for protection)
Jar with lid

METHOD

1. Light the dragon's blood incense and cleanse your tools, ingredients, and workspace. Let the incense burn throughout the spell in a holder.
2. Ground your energies and cast a circle, if it is part of your practice.
3. Gather a photo of each member of your family you want to protect. This could be separate photos or you can use a group photo.
4. On the back of the separate photos, write the person's full name and date of birth. If you're using a group photo, write the names and birth dates of all the people included.
5. Underneath the name, draw the elemental symbol for Fire and the protection rune Elhaz.
6. Add the photos to the jar and, on top, sprinkle the spices and flower petals and add the crystals.
7. Visualize a ring of fire around the jar, forming a wall of fiery protection around it, and say: *"Around the ones I love, I cast a ring of fiery protection, they are shielded from all kinds of negativity and no harm can come from any direction. So mote it be."*
8. Close the lid and, using the hot wax of a black candle, drip the wax around the lid to seal it.
9. Open your circle.
10. Shake the jar regularly to boost its protective energies.

Fire Symbol

Elhaz

Stop an Argument Spell

Best time to practice: During a Waxing Moon, or on a New Moon, Full Moon, or Wednesday

Whether you are arguing with a friend or family member, or your loved ones are arguing among themselves, this spell will help to stop the fighting and replace it with good communication and listening skills, bringing a sense of peace and calm so that a resolution can be sought.

INGREDIENTS
3.5 fl oz (100 ml) water
9 oz (250 g) sugar (to sweeten the relationship)
1 tsp salt (to remove negativity between those arguing)
1 tsp dried lavender, chopped (for peace and calm)
1 tsp dried rosemary, chopped (for a new start)

TOOLS
Cleansing tools
Bowl
1 white candle (for healing)
1 blue candle (for renewal and forgiveness)
Piece of paper and a pen

METHOD

1. Cleanse the ingredients, tools, and workspace.
2. Start by grounding and centering your energies, then casting a circle, if it is part of your practice.
3. On one side of the paper draw the symbol of the throat chakra (below), which is associated with good communication, listening skills, and authentic speech.
4. On the other side of the paper, write the full names of the people arguing (including yourself if you are connected to the fight) nine times for each name across the paper.
5. Turn the paper 90 degrees and, across the names, write: "This argument will stop, here and now. Open up better communication between us, bringing peace and understanding to this argument so a resolution can be found."
6. Pour the water into the bowl and add the salt. Place the paper in the water. Pour enough sugar into the bowl on top of the paper so the water is absorbed.
7. Place the candles into the sugar so they stand upright.
8. Sprinkle the herbs on top of the sugar.
9. Light the candles and repeat the words you wrote on the paper, ending with "*So mote it be.*" Let the candles burn out onto the sugar and herbs.
10. Keep the bowl on your altar until the argument has stopped and been resolved.
11. Open your circle.

Spell to Heal a Rift After an Argument

Best time to practice: On a New Moon, Full Moon, or a Wednesday or Friday

Arguments happen in all relationships, but sometimes these arguments can turn into deep rifts that put strain on our relationships with family and friends. This spell will help to heal this rift and bring you closer together again.

INGREDIENTS

1 tsp fresh lemon balm
(for emotional healing)
1 tsp fresh chamomile (to bring calm)
1 tsp fresh rose petals (to help heal trauma)
1 tsp fresh dandelion leaves (to make peace with each other)

TOOLS

Cleansing tools
Circle casting tools (optional)
1 white dinner candle (for peace and harmony)
Knife
Plate
Lighter or matches

METHOD

1. Cleanse your tools, ingredients, and space.
2. Ground your energies and cast a circle, if it is part of your practice.
3. Take the white candle and cut it into as many segments as there are people involved in the argument or rift. Once separated, pull the wick upward a little for each piece, so each segment can be burned later in the spell. You may need to chop a little bit of the candle off to access the wick, so it can be burned.
4. Arrange the candle pieces so they are as far away from each other as possible on the outside of the plate. Then say: *"At the moment, we are far apart, but we will always be connected by the heart. This spell will move us toward each other, and bring us closer to one another."*
5. Now move the candle pieces from the outside of the plate and stand them up in the middle, putting them as close together as possible.
6. Sprinkle the herbs in layers around the candles, and say: *"I move the candles next to one another to symbolize us coming back together again."*
7. Light the candles, and say: *"The argument/rifts between us is healed, we are reunited, now peace, harmony and togetherness prevails. So mote it be."*
8. Let the candles burn out and open your circle.

Conception Tarot Ritual

This tarot spell has been created to be performed by couples in a stable relationship who need a bit of help with conception. It won't fix any fertility issues but it will give a boost of power to your efforts to conceive, especially to those who have been trying for a baby for a while. This ritual is to be performed together.

TOOLS
Cleansing tools
Circle casting tools (optional)
Tarot deck

METHOD

1. Cleanse the tarot cards and your space.
2. Ground your energies before you begin, then cast a circle, if it is part of your practice.
3. Find a place where you are both comfortable and won't be disturbed.
4. Collect the following tarot cards from the deck and lay them out in this order: Ace of Cups (for new beginnings based on emotions), The Empress (for pregnancy and creation), The Sun (for children and success), Nine of Cups (for fulfillment of wishes), and Ten of Cups (for a happy family.)
5. Sit next to each other so you can both hold the tarot cards and make a connection with the cards. Take your time with this visualization.
6. Hold the Ace of Cups card together. This represents emotional new beginnings. Visualize the excitement you have about conceiving.
7. Next, hold The Empress card together, which represents pregnancy and creation. Use the power of your will to visualize a pregnant tummy growing.
8. Hold The Sun card together, which represents children. Visualize the child you want to conceive and how much love you will feel for them.
9. Hold the Nine of Cups card together, which represents the fulfillment of wishes. Visualize the moment you first hold your baby after its birth.
10. Finally, hold the Ten of Cups card together, which represents a happy family. Visualize yourself in your home together with your baby.
11. When you've finished, hold hands and say these words: *"We have visualized getting pregnant, we will our baby into the world. With our combined energies, our desire to conceive, our child is unfurled. We bring our love and commitment and the energies of these cards, to help us start a family so we can hold our baby in our arms. So mote it be."*
12. Open your circle.

Tea for Better Connections with Loved Ones

If you want to foster a better connection with either friends of family, it is thought that sharing a cup of jasmine tea will help to strengthen your connection, particularly friendships. To make tea for two people, you can use two tea ball strainers, in a teapot, but if you don't have these things, you can use the method below.

INGREDIENTS

Kettle of hot water

3 tsp dried jasmine, or two jasmine tea bags (to strengthen relationships)

2 tsp fresh lavender (to strengthen friendships)

2 tsp dried rose petals (to bring you together in love)

TOOLS

Cleansing tools

Tea ball strainer

2 mugs

METHOD

1. Cleanse your tools, ingredients, and space.
2. Ground your energies.
3. Fill two mugs with hot (but not boiling) water.
4. Add the herbs and petals to a tea ball strainer, place the strainer into the water, and leave to steep for 7–9 minutes. If you don't have jasmine flowers, you could use two jasmine tea bags. Split the bags open and add the contents to the tea strainer before placing into the water.
5. During this time, stir the tea three times in a clockwise direction to attract better connections with the person you are sharing the tea with.
6. As you do, say: *"Bring us closer together, we have come through all weathers. Help to strengthen and better our connection, and the feelings of love and affection. So mote it be."*
7. Pour the tea into the mugs through a tea ball strainer, removing the herbs from the water.
8. Enjoy the tea with your loved one!

Attract New Friends Spell

Best time to practice: During a Waxing Moon or on a New Moon

If you are wanting to make new relationships and forge new friendships in your life, this spell will help to draw good friends toward you.

INGREDIENTS

1 tsp basil (to attract new friends)
1 tsp thyme (to attract true friendship)
1 tsp marjoram (to attract compassionate and understanding friends)

TOOLS

Cleansing tools
Circle casting tools (optional)
Cauldron or heatproof dish
Lighter or matches
Piece of paper and a pen

METHOD

1. Cleanse your ingredients, tools, and space.
2. Start by grounding and centering your energies, then cast a circle, if it is part of your practice.
3. Sprinkle the herbs in your cauldron or heatproof dish.
4. On the piece of paper, write about the friends you would like to attract toward you, the qualities you are looking for in them, and the kind of friendship you want to have. Go into as much detail as possible.
5. When you've finished, roll the paper up and hold it to keep it from unraveling.
6. Holding on to one end of the paper, light the other end. Hold the paper until it has burned down a little but is still far away from your fingers.
7. Place it in your cauldron or heatproof dish on top of the herbs to fully burn out and turn to ash. As it burns, say: *"As my petition burns, I draw toward me the kind of new friends I seek with these words I speak. So mote it be."*
8. Make sure the paper fully burns out and there are only ashes left.
9. Open your circle.
10. Let the ashes fully cool before scooping them up, along with all the herbs. If you live near a moving body of water such as a river, stream, creek, or even the ocean, go to your chosen place and tip the ashes and herbs into the water to symbolize giving your intentions to the universe. Alternatively, wait for a windy day and throw the ashes and herbs into the wind to put your intentions out there.

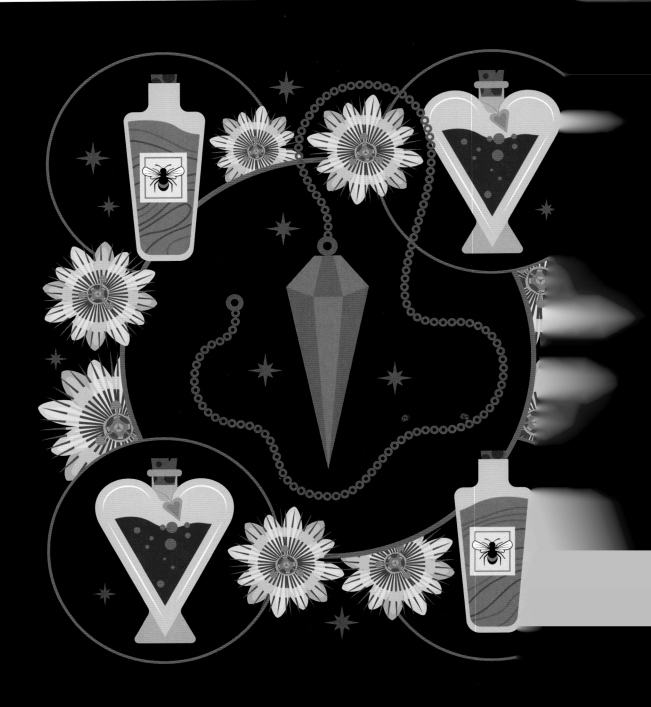

CHAPTER 16

Love & Romantic Relationships

It's fair to say that love spells are among the most popular forms of magick. In this chapter you'll find spells and rituals to strengthen your relationships, attract romantic love and passion, and to help let go of past relationships you may be struggling to move on from.

Clarify a Relationship Ritual

Best time to practice: On a New Moon, Full Moon, or Friday

When we start a new relationship, or are in the initial phases of a relationship, it can be difficult to know if the person is right for us and whether we should carry on seeing them. You need some clarification as to what to do. This pendulum ritual will help to guide you by tapping into your own intuition, bringing out the answers and truths that are already deep inside you.

TOOLS
Cleansing tools
Circle casting tools (optional)
A pendulum (or necklace with a pendant)
Piece of paper and a pen

METHOD

1. Cleanse your tools and workspace.
2. Ground yourself and cast a circle, if it is part of your practice.
3. Make a pendulum board on the piece of paper using the following steps: draw a cross in the middle of the paper that extends near to the edges. On the horizontal line, at each end, write the word "no." At both ends of the vertical line write the word "yes."
4. Turn the paper 45 degrees and draw another cross in the gaps so it now has eight points. At both ends of one line, write the word "maybe," and at both ends of the other, write "rephrase question." This means you need to ask your question in a different way in order to get a more solid answer.
5. Hold your pendulum in your hand for a few moments to connect to its energy.
6. When you're ready, hold your pendulum lightly between your thumb and index finger. Dangle it over the middle of your piece of paper.
7. Ask your first question and watch the way the pendulum moves. It takes time and patience to build up a relationship with your pendant, so the answers might not be as clear when first practicing this form of divination. Keep an open mind and don't come with preconceived ideas about the answers you want, since this could affect the pendulum. You may have to ask your question again if the response is unclear.
8. Continue to ask your questions, giving the pendulum time to respond. How the pendulum moves can offer more information. If the pendulum swings a lot in one direction, it is a definite answer, but if it only moves a little, the answer isn't definite and you can ask more questions to find out why this is.
9. When you have finished, open your circle.

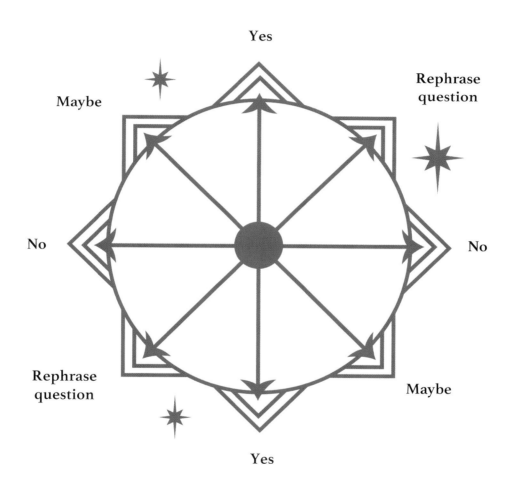

Yes

Rephrase question

Maybe

No

No

Rephrase question

Maybe

Yes

Seduction Oil

Best time to practice: During a Waxing Moon, or on a Full Moon, New Moon, or Friday

This oil will help you to feel more seductive and alluring. Wear it when you want to improve your sex life, when you are looking for a new romantic connection, or when you are dating. It stimulates the senses and opens the heart to desire and love. It can also be added to a bath, in an aromatherapy diffuser, or as a massage oil.

INGREDIENTS
6.5 fl oz (190 ml) base oil such as grapeseed or sunflower oil
2 drops jasmine essential oil (to bring desire)
3 drops patchouli essential oil (to unlock passion within)
3 drops ylang-ylang essential oil (to bring sensuality)
3 drops sandalwood essential oil (for alluring and seductive powers)

TOOLS
Cleansing tools
Dropper bottle

METHOD

1. Cleanse your ingredients, tools, and space.
2. Ground yourself before you start.
3. Take your bottle and add your essential oils.
4. Fill your bottle up with the base oil of your choice.
5. Place the top on the bottle, giving it a good shake to mix the oils together.
6. With your dominant hand, hold the jar and say these words: *"May this oil help me to feel more seductive, in my love life may it be productive. To make me feel more alluring is my desire, enticing, and beguiling powers may I acquire. So mote it be."*
7. Place in the moonlight to charge before use.

Note: Small amounts of essential oils can cause irritation to very sensitive skin, even when diluted. Always perform a patch test when using this recipe for the first time.

Tarot Spell to Attract Romantic Love

Best time to practice: During a Waxing Moon, or on a Full Moon or Friday

At some point in our lives, most of us seek out romantic love and connections. This tarot spell will allow you to open the door to romantic love and enable you to attract this love into all areas of your life. This isn't a spell to make someone fall in love with you, but it creates the right energy for a consensual romantic connection to begin.

INGREDIENTS

1 tsp honey (to bring sweetness)
1 tsp dried pink rose petals (for romantic love)
1 tsp dried lavender buds (for love)
Rose quartz (to attract love)
Rhodonite (to nurture love)

TOOLS

Cleansing tools
Circle casting tools (optional)
Tarot deck
Knife
2 pink candles (for love)
Plate
Piece of paper and a pen
Lighter or matches

METHOD

1. Cleanse your ingredients and tools.
2. Ground your energy and cast a circle, if it is part of your practice.
3. Gather the following tarot cards: The Lovers (for love), Ace of Cups (for new emotional connections), Two of Cups (for partnership and unity).
4. Using a knife, carve your full name into one candle and the name of the person you are romantically interested in into the other candle.
5. Rub a small amount of honey onto both candles.
6. Mix the dried herbs together and sprinkle them onto the plate, in a heart shape.
7. Place the two pink candles inside the heart on the plate.
8. Add the rose quartz and rhodonite to sit inside the heart. Think about the kind of love you wish to attract for yourself.
9. On a piece of paper, draw the symbol of Venus, the planet of love, and add this to the plate between the two candles.
10. Place the tarot cards on or around the plate.
11. Light the candles, concentrate on attracting love between you and the other person, and say: *"I open the doors to romantic love and connection. I welcome in affection. If this is in both of our hearts, may this connection grow and blossom and romantic energy spark. So mote it be."*
12. Concentrate on attracting love between the two people, as represented by the candles.
13. Let the candles burn out and open your circle.

Heal Heartbreak Tea

Heartbreak is painful. This tea can help to heal and strengthen the heart, to support you as you go through it.

INGREDIENTS
Kettle of hot water
1 tsp hawthorn berries
(to heal heartbreak)
1 tsp dried lemon balm
(to lift the spirits)
1 tsp rosemary (to strengthen
the heart)
1 tsp motherwort leaves (to de-stress
and heal the heart)

TOOLS
Cleansing tools
Tea ball strainer
Mug

METHOD
1. Cleanse your tools, ingredients, and space.
2. Start by grounding and centering your energy.
3. Heat water in the kettle until it is hot but not boiling and fill up your mug.
4. Place the herbs in the tea ball strainer and close it up, placing it in the water and allowing to steep for 5-7 minutes. Remove the strainer.
5. Say these words three times: *"May this tea heal the heartbreak I am suffering. So mote it be."*
6. Enjoy your tea.

Note: Rosemary should be avoided by people with epilepsy. All herbal teas must be taken with caution by anyone taking prescribed medication. Check with your medical herbalist or doctor before drinking this tea, and avoid if pregnant.

Love Oil

This oil can attract love into your life and bring strength and passion to existing relationships.

INGREDIENTS
10 fl oz (300 ml) base oil such as
grapeseed or sunflower oil
2 drops jasmine essential oil
(for love)
2 drops lavender essential oil
(for love)
2 drops rose essential oil (for love)
2 drops rosemary essential oil
(for love)

TOOLS
Cleansing tools
Bottle

METHOD
1. Cleanse all your tools and ingredients.
2. Ground your energy.
3. Put two drops of each of the essential oils in the bottle.
4. Fill the rest of the bottle with your chosen oil and give it a shake. As you do, say these words: *"I am a magnet for love, I attract it into my life. As I shake this bottle, I generate energy to supercharge the potency of this oil, it pulls love toward me and attracts love into my life. So mote it be."*
5. Place your oil in the light of the Full Moon (or under its energies if the sky is cloudy) to charge for 2-3 hours. Your oil is ready to use. Apply to the skin or use in spells and rituals to attract love.

Note: Rosemary should be avoided by people with epilepsy. Small amounts of essential oils can cause irritation to very sensitive skin, even when diluted. Always perform a patch test when using this recipe for the first time.

Spell to Repel Unwanted Romantic Attention

Best time to practice: During a Waxing Moon, or on a New Moon, Full Moon, or Saturday

If there is someone in your life who is paying you unwanted (romantic or otherwise) attention, this spell will help to repel and remove them so they leave you alone. This spell is meant as a general deterrent, but if someone is giving you excessive unwanted attention, seek help and take action.

INGREDIENTS

3 rose thorns (for protection against unwanted attention)
1 tsp dried chili (to remove unwanted attention)
1 tsp dried rosemary (to cleanse negative energies associated with unwanted attention)
1 tsp ground nutmeg (to repel unwanted attention)

TOOLS

Cleansing tools
Circle casting tools (optional)
Charcoal disc
Cauldron or heatproof dish
Lighter or matches
Piece of paper and a pen

METHOD

1. Cleanse your tools, ingredients, and space.
2. Take some time to ground yourself and cast a circle, if it is part of your practice.
3. Place the charcoal disc into the cauldron or heatproof dish. Light the charcoal disc until it begins to spark and leave it until it begins to turn white.
4. Sprinkle the rose thorns, dried chili, and rosemary onto the hot charcoal disc.
5. Take a moment to visualize the person giving you unwanted attention.
6. When you're ready, write the name of the person on the paper.
7. Turn the paper 90 degrees and write the words, "I repel your unwanted attention," horizontally across the name until it is completely covered and you can no longer see it.
8. In the middle of the paper, sprinkle the nutmeg to symbolize repelling the unwanted attention. Fold the paper up so that the nutmeg won't fall out. As you do, say these words: *"I repel your unwanted attention, this is my intervention. You will leave me alone, your attentions I will not condone. Take my 'no' for an answer, this is my command, this you will understand. So mote it be."*
9. Take the paper and nutmeg and set it alight, allowing the ashes to fall onto the charcoal disc and the herbs and spices in your cauldron or heatproof dish. Let the paper burn down completely into ashes to symbolize the removal of the unwanted attention.
10. Allow the charcoal disc to cool down fully before disposing of the ashes.
11. Open your circle.

Pouch to Attract Your Perfect Partner

Best time to practice: On a Full Moon or Friday

This spell is perfect for when you are actively looking for a long-term relationship with someone who you are very well matched with. It helps to attract the kind of partner who ticks all the boxes.

INGREDIENTS

1 tsp ground cinnamon
(to attract love)
1 tsp dried basil, chopped (to attract your partner)
1 tsp dried thyme, chopped (to attract true love)
Dried red rose petals, chopped (to heal the heart and induce love)
Rose quartz (to manifest love)
Lapis lazuli (to give clarity of sight in love and offer guidance)
Clear quartz (to support your intentions)

TOOLS

Cleansing tools
Circle casting tools (optional)
Piece of paper and a pen
Red fabric pouch with a tie
Lighter or matches
Cauldron or heatproof dish

METHOD

1. Gather all your ingredients together and cleanse them.
2. Start by grounding and centering your energies, then cast a circle, if it is part of your practice.
3. Write down the characteristic of your ideal partner. Be incredibly specific about the person you want to attract, including details of their ideal qualities, temperament, physical appearance, morals, and interests. Be honest about what you are and aren't looking for so that you can attract your perfect partner.
4. Fold the paper up and hold it in your hand. Take a moment to connect to your intentions.
5. Take the pouch and add the herbs and crystals to it.
6. Take the paper and burn it, letting it turn to ash in the cauldron or heatproof dish.
7. When the paper is completely turned to ash, add it to the pouch.
8. As you do, say this incantation: "*Let my perfect partner find their way to me, bring them closer to me, this is my guarantee. The qualities I look for, they will be fulfilled, I'll find the perfect person for me and a strong relationship we shall build. So mote it be.*"
9. Open your circle.
10. Keep the pouch near your bed until the spell is complete.

Ritual to Let Go of a Relationship

Best time to practice: During a Waning Moon

This ritual can be used when a relationship is over but emotions remain. It will help you to clear away the energy that still forms some kind of connection between you both so you can fully let go of the relationship.

TOOLS
Cleansing tools
Circle casting tools (optional)
Photo of the person you want to let go of, a letter or note from them, or their name and birthday on a piece of paper
Lighter or matches
Cauldron or heatproof dish

METHOD

1. Before you begin, cleanse you tools.
2. Ground yourself and your energies, then cast a circle, if it is part of your practice.
3. Take the photo, letter, note, or piece of paper and, on the back of it, write about the aspects of the relationship that still remain and which you want to let go of. Be as specific as you can, given the space you have available.
4. When finished, burn the photo in a cauldron or heatproof dish.
5. As it burns, repeat this incantation: *"The fire breaks the bonds that still exist, in letting go I must persist. I let go of all the things that remain, in doing so, I release my pain. So mote it be!"*
6. Open your circle.
7. Collect the ashes that are left and tip them into running water such as a river, stream, or even the ocean, to symbolize letting go and removing all traces of them from your life. Alternatively, if you can't use natural running water, turn on the tap in your sink and wash the ashes away.

PART III

Correspondence

Many Witches use correspondence to help them choose the ingredients to use in their spell work. Everything in the world has its own distinct energy, which connects it to specific types of magick. Guided by this specific energy, magickal correspondence list items such as herbs, spices, crystals, resins, and flowers, and the magickal energy they align with, such as love, protection, happiness, health, and peace. Using correspondence can help you create your own spells or rework the spells in this book to align with your specific intentions or better suit your needs.

These correspondence also include the magickal meanings of Moon phases and the times of the day, which can be used to help time your magick. Other aspects of spell crafting such as the magickal significance of different colors and the meaning of runes can also be incorporated into your spell work.

It's worth noting that correspondence can vary a little between different countries and cultures, so use your intuition when choosing spell ingredients and timings and use what feels right to you and your practice.

Herbs & Citrus

BASIL: Protection, love, lust, wealth, psychic abilities.
BAY: Protection, purification, success, prosperity, wishes.
BERGOMOT: Prosperity, good fortune.
CATNIP: Love, cat magick, happiness, beauty.
CEDAR: Healing, purification, psychic abilities, money, protection.
CHAMOMILE: Healing, happiness, calm, sleep, money, purification.
CILANTRO (CORIANDER): Love, lust, healing, protection.
CLOVER: Money, luck, success, protection, fidelity.
COMFREY: Travel, protection, money.
DANDELION: Healing, success, divination.
DILL: Money, love, protection, luck, lust.
LAVENDER: Peace, calm, protection, love, sleep.
LEMON: Protection, purification, banishing, love.
LEMON BALM: Success, calm, healing, purification, longevity.
MINT: Healing, protection, prosperity, money, luck.
MUGWORT: Psychic abilities, protection, dream work, strength.
NETTLE: Protection, warding, strength, healing.
ORANGE: Prosperity, psychic abilities, good fortune, cleansing, luck.
OREGANO: Money, health, love, peace, courage.
PARSLEY: Purification, spirit communication, protection, good luck, fertility.
PATCHOULI: Grounding, abundance, money, desire.
PEPPERMINT: Psychic abilities, cleansing, sleep, clarity, prosperity.
ROSEMARY: Protection, mental powers, purification, healing, love, banishing.
RUE: Breaking hexes, psychic abilities, good health, healing.
SAGE: Purification, protection, wisdom, spiritual enhancement.
TARRAGON: Protection, confidence, courage, banishing.
THYME: Purification, good health, love, healing, psychic abilities, courage.
YARROW: Love, courage, psychic abilities.
VALERIAN: Calm, aids sleep, protection, love.
VERVAIN: Prosperity, sleep, love, protection, peace.
WORMWOOD: Protection, banishing.

Spices

ALLSPICE: Money, luck, protection, prosperity, success.
BLACK PEPPER: Protection, banishing.
CARAWAY: Protection, psychic abilities, money, love, friendship.
CAYENNE PEPPER: Banishing, removing obstacles, reversing hexes, purification.
CHILI PEPPER: Protection, passion, sexual desire, male fertility, hex breaking.
CINNAMON: Protection, power, psychic abilities, drawing toward, strength, lust, success.
CLOVE: Protection, money, love, prosperity.
CUMIN: Protection, fidelity, prevents threat, peace.
FENNEL: Protection, purification, wards off evil spirits, courage, strength.
MARJORAM: Prosperity, protection, love, happiness.
NUTMEG: Luck, money, fidelity, power, success, psychic abilities.
SALT: Protection, purification, cleansing, grounding.
STAR ANISE: Protection, luck, psychic awareness.
TURMERIC: Purification, abundance, happiness, fertility.

Resins

<u>BENZOIN</u>: Purification, confidence, calm, love.
<u>COPAL</u>: Protection, grounding, love.
<u>DRAGON'S BLOOD</u>: Protection, banishing, power, good fortune, love.
<u>FRANKINCENSE</u>: Protection, psychic abilities, consecration.
<u>GUM ARABIC</u>: Protection, platonic love, raises vibrations.
<u>MYRRH</u>: Purification, healing, banishing.

Flowers

CALENDULA: Protection, dreams, manifestation, abundance.
CARNATION: Protection, breaking hexes, healing, strength.
DAISY: Divination, love, happiness.
ELDERFLOWER: Healing, good health, protection, purification.
GERANIUM: Love, protection, balance, fertility, healing.
HIBISCUS: Love, lust, passion, sexual desire, psychic abilities.
HONEYSUCKLE: Money, prosperity, luck, protection, psychic abilities.
HYACINTH: Love, happiness, protection, abundance, joy.
JASMINE: Money, love, prophetic dreams, protection.
LILY: Protection, attract love, repel hexes.
MALLOW: Attraction, protection, positive energies.
PASSIONFLOWER: Calm, peace, sleep, friendship, healing.
POPPY: Love, fertility, money, sleep.
PRIMROSE: Protection, healing, good luck, prosperity.
ROSE: Love, romance, healing, love divination.
SUNFLOWER: Happiness, good luck, truth, protection, good health.

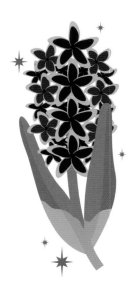

Crystals

AMAZONITE: Calm, peace, courage, confidence, emotional balance, strength.

AMBER: Abundance, healing, success, vitality, joy.

AMETHYST: Protection, psychic abilities, dreams, calm, health, communication.

AQUAMARINE: Prosperity, health, joy, courage, reduces stress.

AVENTURINE: Prosperity, luck, creativity, balances emotions.

BLACK OBSIDIAN: Protection, self-control, cleansing, strength, soul healing.

BLACK TOURMALINE: Protection, grounding, eliminates negativity, emotional cleansing.

BLUE LACE AGATE: Communication, calm, emotional healing, personal growth.

CARNELIAN: Prosperity, courage, success, protection, ambition.

CITRINE: Prosperity, abundance, health, joy, optimism, friendships.

CLEAR QUARTZ: Manifestation, balance.

FLUORITE: Protection, psychic abilities, mental clarity, emotional detoxification.

HEMATITE: Protection, grounding, memory, concentration.

JET: Protection, grounding, relieves anxiety.

LABRADORITE: Protection, transformation, intuition, personal growth.

LEPIDOLITE: Inner peace, mood stabilizing, soothing.

MALACHITE: Protection, transformation, spiritual growth, emotional healing.

MOONSTONE: Enhancing intuition, psychic awareness, new beginnings, balancing.

RED JASPER: Strength, courage, protection, stamina.

RHODOCROSITE: Compassion, healing past wounds, emotional healing.

RHODONITE: Emotional balance, love, affection, sex, nurture, self-love.

ROSE QUARTZ: Love, beauty, harmony, relationships.

SELENITE: Cleansing, recharging, intuition, wisdom, protection.

SMOKY QUARTZ: Grounding, protection, dispels fear and negativity, mental clarity.

SODALITE: Grounding, communication, calm, inner peace.

TIGER'S EYE: Protection, prosperity, good luck, confidence, strength, courage.

TURQUOISE: Protection, abundance, wealth, luck.

Colors

BLACK: Protection, banishing, binding, breaking hexes, spirit work, acceptance.
BLUE: Peace, healing, calm, renewal, communication, wisdom, self-expression.
GOLD: Wealth, attraction, abundance, masculine energy.
GREEN: Luck, fertility, growth, abundance, money, change.
ORANGE: Success, positivity, creativity, confidence, ambition.
PINK: Sensuality, compassion, love, beauty, self-love, romance.
PURPLE: Intuition, psychic abilities, divination, spirituality.
RED: Courage, assertiveness, energy, passion, power, strength, sex.
SILVER: Intuition, Moon magick, awareness, feminine energy, spirituality.
WHITE: Purification, cleansing, healing, blessings.
YELLOW: Action, joy, abundance, communication, happiness, memory, enthusiasm.

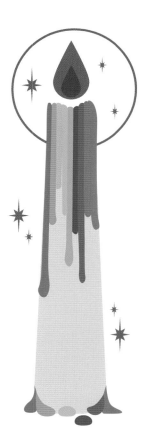

Days of the Week

<u>MONDAY</u>: Emotions, intuition, dreams, reconciliation, spirituality, cleaning, Moon magick, healing.
<u>TUESDAY</u>: Passion, banishing, strength, courage, banishing fear, sex, motivation, energy, ambition.
<u>WEDNESDAY</u>: Communication, learning, creativity, knowledge, travel, memory, confidence.
<u>THURSDAY</u>: Luck, wealth, abundance, career and work, success, prosperity, optimism.
<u>FRIDAY</u>: Love, beauty, lust, art, fertility, birth, romance, sex, relationships.
<u>SATURDAY</u>: Banishing, protection, cleansing, purification.
<u>SUNDAY</u>: Growth, health, empowerment, vitality, removing barriers, material wealth.

Time of the Day

<u>SUNRISE</u>: New beginnings, fresh energies, cleansing, purification, healing, study.
<u>DAYTIME</u>: Expansion, intelligence, leadership.
<u>MIDDAY</u>: Power, health, money, success, strength, opportunity, vitality, courage.
<u>SUNSET</u>: Truth, release, letting go, closure, breaking bad habits.
<u>NIGHT-TIME</u>: Self-development, awareness, healing old wounds, releasing stress.
<u>MIDNIGHT</u>: Banishing, healing, power, self-enhancement, divination.

Moon Phases

NEW MOON: New beginnings, intentions, manifestation, protection, grounding, rest, rejuvenation, possibilities.

WAXING CRESCENT: Change, growth, fertility, positivity, attraction, rebuilding, self-confidence.

FIRST QUARTER: Growth, alignment, creativity, decisions, reflection, action.

WAXING GIBBOUS: Refinement of intentions, adjusting, attraction, patience.

FULL MOON: Power, energy, charging, cleaning, release, healing, intuition.

WANING GIBBOUS: Evaluation, nurture yourself and others, release, receive, gratitude.

THIRD QUARTER: Forgiveness, letting go, banishing bad habits, elimination, cleansing, breaking hexes.

WANING CRESCENT: Letting go, wisdom, surrender, self-care, rest, restore, intuition.

Runes

FEHU: Wealth, luck, material wealth, prosperity, fortune.
URUZ: Strength, endurance, courage, vitality, health.
THURISAZ: Defense, attack, strength, danger, boundaries.
ANSUZ: Communication, knowledge, insight, inspiration.
RAIDHO: Travel, movement, progress, journey, evolution.
KAUNAN: Knowledge, tradition, insight, experience, enlightenment.
GEBO: Partnerships, talents, luck, fortune, exchanges, generosity, gift.
WUNJO: Blessings, joy, comfort, success, harmony, pleasure, prosperity.
HAGAIAZ: Destruction, uncontrolled forces, change, power.
NAUDHIZ: Survival, resistance, need, endurance, restriction, lacking.
ISAZ: Deception, frustration, delay, blocks, introspection, waiting.
JERA: Rewards, cycles, endings and beginnings, prosperity, abundance, growth, peace.
EIHWAZ: Strength, protection, stability, reliability, connection.
PERTHRO: Destiny, foresight, mysteries, fortune, mysticism, unknown, divination.
ELHAZ: Protection, defense, courage, ward off evil, awakening, instincts.
SOWILO: Success, happiness, abundance, renewal, vitality.
TIWAZ: Justice, honor, bravery, strength, leadership, victory.
BERKANAN: Fertility, new starts, birth, creativity, growth.
EHWAZ: Movement, trust, loyalty, progress, harmony.
MANNAZ: Community, relationships, morals, values, humanity.
LAGUZ: Instinct, insight, intuitions, healing, dreams, subconscious.
INGWAZ: Fertility, inner growth, potential, peace.
OTHAIAN: Inheritence, abundance, spiritual growth, legacy, heritage.
DAGAZ: Awakenings, consciousness, breakthrough, new cycles, clarity.

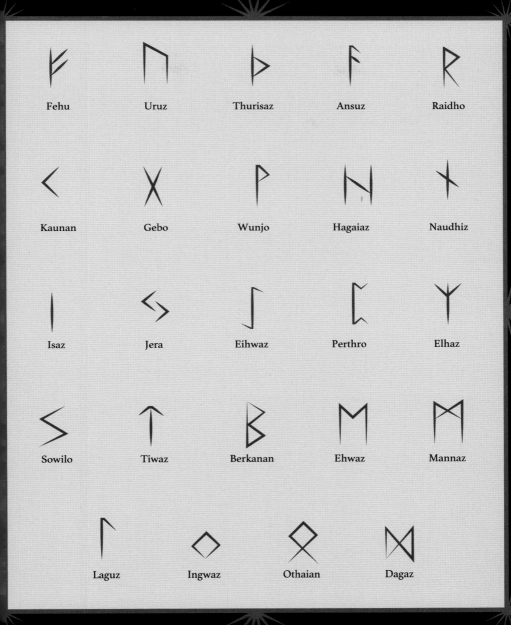

Fehu   Uruz   Thurisaz   Ansuz   Raidho

Kaunan   Gebo   Wunjo   Hagaiaz   Naudhiz

Isaz   Jera   Eihwaz   Perthro   Elhaz

Sowilo   Tiwaz   Berkanan   Ehwaz   Mannaz

Laguz   Ingwaz   Othaian   Dagaz

Further Reading

For those who are interested in expanding their practice further and wish to read other spell books, these are some of my favorites:

Skye Alexander, *The Modern Witchcraft Spell Book*
Pamela Ball, *The Book of Spells*
Bridget Bishop, *The Crystal Magic Spell Book*
Frankie Castanea, *Spells for Change*
Cheralyn Darcey, *The Book of Herb Spells*
Ember Grant, *The Book of Crystal Spells*
Ambrosia Hawthorn, *The Spell Book for New Witches*
Roger J. Horne, *The Witch's Art of Incantation: Spoken Charms, Spells & Curses in Folk Witchcraft*
Judika Illes, *The Element Encyclopaedia of 5000 Spells*
Graham King, *The British Book of Spells and Charms*
Claude Lecouteux, *Traditional Magic Spells for Protection and Healing*
Wren Maple, *The Thrifty Witch's Book of Simple Spells*
Madam Pamita, *Candle Magic*
Silja, *The Green Wiccan Spell Book*
Lucya Starza, *Candle Magic: A Witch's Guide to Spells and Rituals*

Other books available by Lindsay Squire

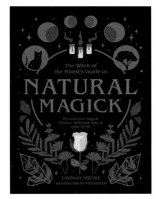

Natural Magick
978-0711266834

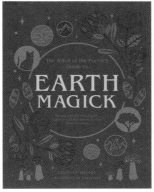

Earth Magick
978-0711271722

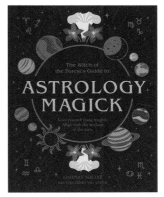

Astrology Magick
978-0711277182

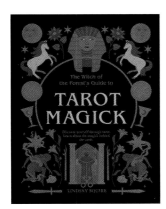

Tarot Magick
978-0711280649

Tarot Magick Deck
978-0711281035

Witchcraft: A Graphic History
978-0711295254

Index

Acknowledgments

A spell book has been a book I have wanted to write about for a long time and it's been wonderful to realize this dream. Writing it has been such an incredible experience and my hope it that it will provide help and inspiration to Witches of all levels of experience, but particularly those at the start of their Witchcraft journey.

First and foremost, I want to express my heartfelt thanks to you, the reader, for taking the time, energy, and money to choose this book and I sincerely hope that you find it useful. I am filled with so much gratitude for your support, and it is thanks to you that I have been able to realize my dream to become a published author. I could not have done it without you!

I would like to acknowledge the extraordinary debt I owe to my incredible family, especially my mum, dad, sister Rachael, and auntie Carol, who have always been there for me, encouraging me throughout the good and difficult times. They have been by my side throughout this project and I'm eternally grateful for their constant and unwavering love. They have been a pillar of encouragement and whose support means the world to me. I have always admired and looked up to Rachael's knowledge of the craft and she has been an incredible source of inspiration as I wrote this book, providing a listening ear and someone who I could talk about ideas with.

The experience of writing this book has been made more amazing because of the support from everyone at Leaping Hare Press and Quarto, particularly Monica and Chloe. Their belief in me has given me more confidence in myself than they will ever know and I am eternally grateful for their patience, encouragement, and faith in my abilities. I'd also like to thank Viki (@forensicsandflowers), the most amazing illustrator who has made this book come alive with her creations.